W9-CPE-811

2 95

SYLVIA SIDNEY
NEEDLEPOINT BOOK

Sylvia Sidney
with
Alfred Allan Lewis

SYLVIA SIDNEY NEEDLEPOINT BOOK

VNR VAN NOSTRAND REINHOLD COMPANY
NEW YORK   CINCINNATI   TORONTO   LONDON   MELBOURNE

I am grateful to Joan Perry for her invaluable help with the black-and-white photography and, most of all, to Jody, who understands—almost everything.

Van Nostrand Reinhold Company Regional Offices:
New York Cincinnati Chicago Millbrae Dallas

Van Nostrand Reinhold Company International Offices:
London Toronto Melbourne

Copyright © 1968 by Sylvia Sidney
Library of Congress Catalog Card Number: 68-22738

ISBN 0-442-11329-3 cloth
0-442-27884-5 paper

All rights reserved. No part of this work covered by the copyright hereon may be reproduced or used in any form or by any means—graphic, electronic, or mechanical, including photocopying, recording, taping, or information storage and retrieval systems—without written permission of the publisher. Manufactured in the United States of America.

Designed by Emilio Squeglio
Type set by Graphic Arts Typographers, Inc.

Published by Van Nostrand Reinhold Company
A Division of Litton Educational Publishing, Inc.
450 West 33rd Street, New York, N.Y. 10001

Published simultaneously in Canada by
Van Nostrand Reinhold Ltd.

16 15 14 13 12 11 10

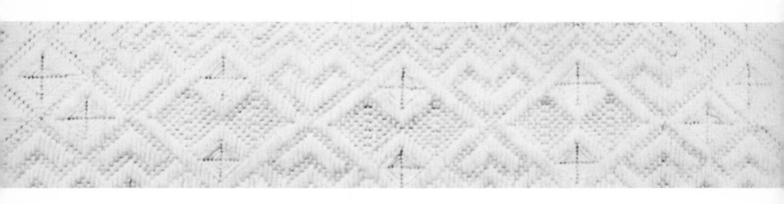

Contents

The author and friends. Sticking out his tongue is Ch. Pug Pens Captain Midnight.

Introduction

People are forever asking me why I took up needlepoint. I might reply with the old adage that idle hands do the devil's handiwork—except that when I have made a terrible error in a design on which I have been hard at work, it seems that busy hands also can do the devil's handiwork. Whichever may be true, my hands have always been full —with play scripts, pugs, or canvases, and generally all three at once.

Actually, needlepoint was just a logical step in the progression of knitting, sewing, embroidering, and the like with which I have been engaged ever since I can remember. I believe that, with the careful application of a few basic rules, anyone who has ever sewn on a button or knitted a simple muffler can learn to do what looks like the most complicated piece of petit or gros point. It involves no more than daring to take one step after another. This, in a manner of speaking, is what my book is all about. The story of my life could be told in the taking of those steps. If it were possible for me to recall all of the things I have made for people I have loved, you would have the auto-biography of Sylvia Sidney.

It all began when I was seven years old and my grandmother taught me how to knit a washcloth. From then on I was hooked on the needle. Through all the years, when I was studying to be an actress and work-ing in my first Broadway shows and in films in Hollywood, I was constantly sewing or knitting. There was a time when I made not only my own clothes but, on numerous occasions, those of my friends as well. One night, I remember, Judy Garland came to my house for dinner and extravagantly admired the pair of Chinese-style silk lounging pajamas I was wearing. Before she could blink an eye, I whipped out my tape measure and took her measurements. I bought some lovely black shantung with gold threading and, on her next visit, presented Judy with her own copy of the pajamas.

But for some reason or other, the sewing machine gave me very little satisfaction. Perhaps it was because I couldn't carry one around in a tote bag and take it out while waiting for a plane, or a cue to make an entrance in a play, or during the long hours spent on movie sets be-tween scenes. In Hollywood, along with the productions of *Street Scene, Trail of the Lonesome Pine, Dead End, You Only Live Once,* and others, there were my personal productions of sweaters, scarves, neck-ties, afghans, suits, and hats intended for relatives, friends, and the children of friends.

I returned to New York in 1938 to be with my husband, Luther Adler, whose career as an actor kept him in the East. Never having been one to tolerate idleness for long, I did two things. I accepted the leading role in Irwin Shaw's play, *The Gentle People,* which co-starred Franchot Tone and featured Elia Kazan, Sam Jaffe, Karl Malden, and

Lee J. Cobb. At the same time, I began to shop around for a house in the country—I have always had the typical New Yorker's desire to spend as much time as possible out of my native city. I found a very old farmhouse set on 120 acres of land in Flemington, New Jersey. It was ideal, being within commuting distance, so Luther and I could get to our jobs in the theater. And it was in only a slight state of disrepair. If you have seen or read *Mr. Blandings Builds His Dream House* or *George Washington Slept Here*, you can translate my last statement fairly accurately. The property was known throughout the area as the Bank Farm. At first I assumed that it had belonged to people named "Bank." I soon learned the truth. It had been in receivership so often that everybody had forgotten the name of the original owner and simply referred to it as belonging to the bank.

Although Luther thought it impossible, I was determined to restore the house and make a beautiful home of it. As with all old houses, the work constituted a voyage of discovery. We found that the oldest part of the house dated from 1780, the newest from 1810. In the process of putting in electricity, plumbing, and central heating, none of which it had, we uncovered wonderful old cupboards and fireplaces with fine mantels that had been walled up for many years. Seeing all the beauty of the original house appear, I decided that we should maintain as much of the authentic period feeling as possible, both in the structure and the furnishings. New windows had to be handcrafted to duplicate the old ones that were still there. When I wasn't acting, I was busy scraping and refinishing antique country furniture.

When the work on the house was done, and the furniture ready, we moved in. Covering the bare floors was the next order of business, and I gave it a great deal of thought. Because they would be in keeping with the rest of the house, I decided on hooked rugs. But the ones I found in stores were either not right or prohibitively expensive. There seemed to be only one solution. I would have to follow in the steps of the first inhabitants of Bank Farm and make them myself. I had never hooked a rug before, but I thought this was as good a time as any to start. *The Gentle People* had just closed, and I was overjoyed to discover that I was pregnant. I had the whole of the summer and autumn to wait for the baby—and to learn how to make a rug.

I got a fairly good idea of the mechanics of hooking by reading all the books on the subject I could find. But those modern techniques were not sufficient to my needs. I wanted rugs made precisely in the manner of the eighteenth century. I began to search the great museums and galleries of New York for examples. At last, through The Metropolitan Museum of Art, which has a wing filled with Early American domestic treasures, I found a lady who knew all there was to know about hooking rugs—she was the person entrusted with the job of repairing those owned by the Museum. She filled out what I had learned from books and taught me the refinements of the craft. She taught me that one of the best backings is monk's cloth, and that there are many sources of materials besides the usual supply stores. For instance, one can cut old clothes (or, for that matter, any fabric) with desirable colors into strips to be woven in, and bleach them to obtain subtle, commercially unprocurable tones for shading. I was soon searching out second-hand clothes and Army-Navy stores for interesting materials.

My first attempt was a rug for our bar. Learning from my mistakes and feeling bolder, I next embarked upon a runner for the winding stairway that led up to our guest rooms. On the risers of the steps I worked in the names of good friends and relatives, with a symbol for each. Clifford Odets, the late playwright, was passionate about music: alongside his name I placed a series of notes from Beethoven's *Fifth*. There were the scales of justice for our lawyer, Arthur Krim, and an orchid for my mother-in-law. The step devoted to Dr. Albert Sabin, my cousin (who was later to become famous for his discovery of the polio vaccine named after him), featured a swirl of tiny bacteria. These designs were seen as one mounted the stairs; looking down from the top, across the treads, one viewed a sea of flowers that seemed to be an extension of the garden.

Having mastered the art of hooking rugs, I felt rather self-confident, and in this frame of mind I conceived a new project for the house. One of the most exciting pieces of furniture we had bought was an original, signed Duncan Phyffe dining room table. After a long search, we finally found a set of very old, very good copies of Duncan Phyffe chairs to go with it. They were upholstered with a dingy material of no intrinsic value. The job I set for myself was to make new covers to match the pattern of the linen dining room drapes, a copy of an eighteenth-century design of tiny, delicately hued flowers scattered on a pale blue background. I decided to work the chair covers in needlepoint.

I had done a little embroidery and even tried my hand at some packaged needlepoint cushions and slippers. To tell the truth, it had not excited me very much. But to do chair covers was different—it was a major project for a house I loved more and more with each day's labor on it.

I cannot imagine what made me believe that the large, free technique of hooking was preparation for the subtleties of needlepoint, but somehow I did. Actually, there is almost no relationship between the two aside from the fact that both utilize a backing. In hooking you measure by inches rather than counting meshes (or threads), as in needlepoint. But there is one thing I learned in hooking that I carried over into the new work: it has to do with color. Color in needlepoint is far more controlled and, consequently, realistic. Yet, I was able to incorporate into it rug toning techniques such as adding touches of red in large areas of green to give them life and kick. Working on the rugs taught me never to be afraid of color. This has been of tremendous value in making my own designs.

When I was in the hospital giving birth to my son, Jody, the canvases for the chairs were being prepared. I used the period of my confinement to find out all I could about how to do them. I fear this made me a terrible disappointment to the nurses. They were expecting a glamourous actress, complete with the frilly negligees and satin sheets that are supposedly standard movie-star equipment. What they got was a lady in a plain cotton wrapper, with glasses on the tip of her nose, poring over a bedful of books about needlepoint.

I never had a lesson on it. I picked up everything I know by studying the extremely informative volumes that have been written on the subject (see the Bibliography). Books and trial and error, or what I call "fumble and fuss," were my teachers.

As soon as I returned home, I started to work on the chairs. I used a mono-canvas of sixteen threads to the inch, and did the entire design in the easy Tent (or Continental) Stitch, which was the only formula I dared undertake. Encouraged by the results, I ventured to take another tentative step and worked a piece on penelope canvas. For this I used the Half-Cross Stitch.

This simple beginning was enough to win me over completely to needlepoint. Ever since, nothing else has so gratified my need to keep creatively busy between scenes when I am acting, and between plays when I am not. Many years passed and many pillows, purses, rugs, and slippers were behind me before I summoned up the courage to try my hand at designing and executing my own drawings on a canvas. But with each piece I did, I learned something new, and each was a small step forward.

I have written this book for the needleworker who is at the same point I was at when I did those dining room chairs and became enamored of a craft that has given me endless pleasure. It is for the person ready to take that next small step that this book begins.

1. A Rose and a Prayer

As far as needle and thread went, the sixteen years following my son's birth and my first discovery of the pleasures of needlepoint passed uneventfully enough. I continued to make a large assortment of hooked rugs and knitted articles for a variety of friends and relatives. In needlepoint, I worked on a multitude of canvases of different gauges, both mono and penelope, and mastered several new stitches. I never departed from the patterns and materials that I could obtain in a regular needlework shop. Occasionally I altered a design slightly to make it a little more personal, but I never dared do more than that.

The turning point came in 1955. My good friend, Don Loper, had just bought a new house in California. Don is one of Hollywood's finest dress designers, and a man of impeccable taste. A glance at even a partial list of his grateful customers shows his ability to satisfy the couturial needs of a group of ladies of wildly diversified tastes—among them are Ginger Rogers, Lena Horne, Connie Francis, Ella Fitzgerald, Irene Dunne, Pearl Bailey, Natalie Wood, and last (but often not least difficult), Sylvia Sidney.

I met Don sometime in the early thirties. Neither of us remember how or where, and it has become a standing joke with us to see who can invent the most extravagantly outlandish circumstances for that meeting. What I do recall vividly is the first time that he designed some clothes for me. There are few women without figure problems, and Hollywood stars are certainly no exceptions. Mine was having a bosom in a pre-Jane Russell era. During the initial fitting, I said sheepishly, "Don, I have a problem. You see, I have a bosom."

He replied crisply, "You'd have a worse problem if you didn't have one."

Is it any wonder he became very dear to me? For the first time in years, a designer was structuring clothes for me, instead of restructuring me for them.

In early 1955 I was living in New York, but I was due on the West Coast in the autumn for a television show. Don was designing my costumes. He would be ready to move into his new house about the time I arrived—and it was also the time of his birthday. I pondered for a long time over the right gift to take him.

One day a friend and I went to The Pierpont Morgan Library to see its beautiful collection of illuminated manuscripts. The stately marble halls of that institution must still be trembling from the jubilant shout

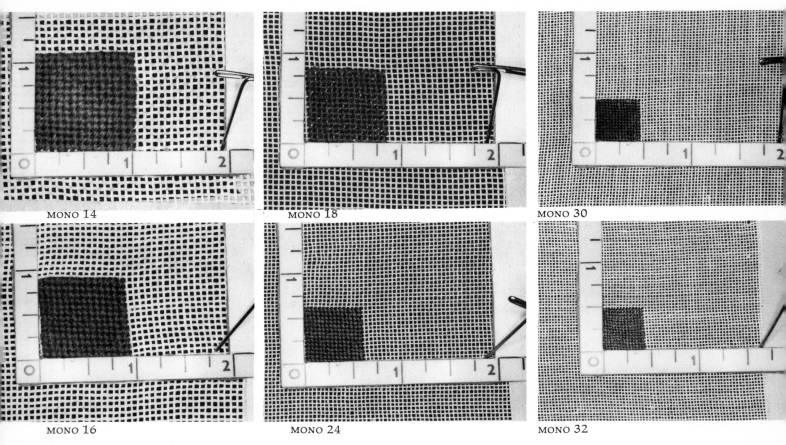

MONO 14 · MONO 18 · MONO 30

MONO 16 · MONO 24 · MONO 32

There are two basic types of canvas used in needlepoint: mono and penelope. Penelope is a double-mesh canvas: there are two threads to every one in a similar mono-canvas. Canvas sizes are given in gauge, or the number of threads per inch. For example, a mono 12 has twelve threads per inch; a penelope 12-24 has twenty-four (twelve double) threads per inch. An advantage of penelope canvas is that you can stitch on either double or single threads, as shown in the illustrations.

I gave when I came upon a particularly lovely page from a twelfth-century Bible. I knew Don would love it too, and it suddenly occurred to me that I could work something similar in needlepoint. The whole composition took shape in my mind. The moving prayer of St. Francis of Assisi had long been a source of inspiration to Don. There could be no more appropriate text for my piece than the words of the twelfth-century saint:

Lord make me the instrument of thy peace;
Where there is hatred, let me sow love;
Where there is injury, pardon;
Where there is doubt, faith;
Where there is despair, hope;
Where there is darkness, light;
And where there is sadness, joy.

O Divine Master, grant that I may not
So much seek to be consoled as to console;
To be understood as to understand;
To be loved as to love;
For it is in giving that we receive;
It is in pardoning that we are pardoned;
And it is in dying that we are born
　　　　To Eternal life.

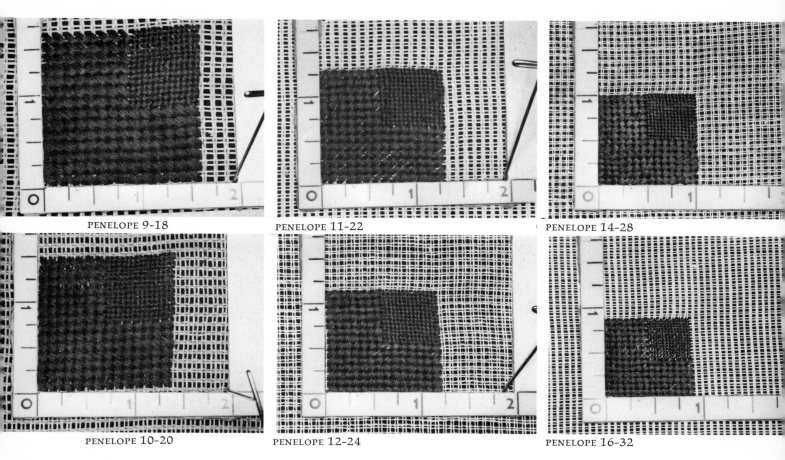

PENELOPE 9-18

PENELOPE 11-22

PENELOPE 14-28

PENELOPE 10-20

PENELOPE 12-24

PENELOPE 16-32

I knew exactly how I wanted to execute it—every detail down to the kind of canvas, the materials, and the colors. The whole piece would be done in Diagonal Tent Stitch on a fine linen mono-canvas; although most canvas material is cotton, linen has always been my preference, because I find that it works more easily and gives a better backing for blocking. I wanted the gauge to be between twenty-four and twenty-eight threads per inch so that the stitchery would be quite fine, simulating an illuminated page as closely as possible. For the same reason, I decided to use silk and gold threads, which in itself was an exciting challenge, since I had never done any needlepoint with these threads. Until then I had always used wool.

I could hardly wait to get to a needlework shop so I could have my ideas transcribed onto a canvas. I generally dealt with a shop on the Coast, but I was too impatient to wait for the materials to be sent to me—or even long enough to ask friends who did needlepoint to recommend a place in New York. I wrote out the prayer, carefully sketched what I wanted the canvas to look like, and went to the first needlework shop I found. The people there listened very attentively and assured me there would be no difficulties. It was simply a case of being patient while they gathered all the necessary materials and prepared the canvas. In those days, stores didn't carry a very wide range of stock. Needlepoint had not yet become the popular pastime it is today.

I had a great deal of preparation to do for the plays in which I was

DIAGONAL TENT STITCH

see page 86

13

going to appear that summer in stock. I was playing Rosemary in *Picnic*, which I had not acted in before, and Mrs. Manningham in *Angel Street*, which I had not done for many years. The weeks passed swiftly. Rehearsals were due to begin shortly, and I wanted a good start on the prayer. Finally, just as I was beginning to get a little anxious, the canvas and materials were ready.

I picked them up at the shop and raced home to get to work. For the next few weeks, when I was not memorizing lines, I was doing the prayer. During the rehearsals for *Picnic*, when I got down on my knees to beg Howard, my fellow, to marry me, I was clutching the St. Francis prayer. Come to think of it, it was rather appropriate.

I did countless stitches, finishing the gold cross at the top and dozens of letters. Then, something an agent once said was brought home vividly. "Sylvia," he had warned me, "before you sign any contract, read every single word—and then still pray." In this case, I should read the prayer. I was more than halfway through the work, when I came to the word *receive*, it looked very peculiar. It should have! It was spelled *recive*.

"Well," I thought, "it's a stupid mistake, but I can fix it easily enough. I'll just stick in the *e*." Alas, it simply could not be done. After vainly trying for hours, I began to wish I had never learned how to spell.

The sad truth is that lettering in needlepoint is the same as lettering in printing. Every space—in this case, mesh—must be counted and planned for carefully. The alternative is a design with margins and spaces that are haphazardly uneven.

I fumbled and foolishly fussed with the prayer. I picked out the silk threads so often that all I could think of was Whittier's admonition, "Pluck one thread and the web ye mar." For a moment I considered leaving the word as it was. Let people laugh and dismiss it as another dumb mistake by another dumb actress.

I re-marked the canvas and then re-re-marked it. I went to every book of instructions I owned, but it was no use. If you have ever worked with a canvas of twenty-eight threads per inch, you can imagine what it was like by three in the morning. It was the worst mess I had made since my grandmother first taught me how to use a knitting needle. In spite of the hour, I decided to call on my son for help. (His father, Luther Adler, and I had been divorced for several years.)

Mathematics was and still is Jody's forte. (As a matter of fact, he was then only one year away from M.I.T.) I explained the problem, and threw myself on the mercy of my tousle-haired and sleepy-eyed son. He studied the canvas for a moment. Then he turned to me and said, patiently and reasonably, "It's simple, mom. You work it all out on graph paper."

Graph paper! It was three in the morning, and I hadn't seen a sheet of graph paper since I was in the seventh grade.

Jody was more patient and reasonable than ever. He just brought me a pad of the paper. It proved to be the perfect solution! The lines and tiny squares could be made to correspond exactly to the threads and meshes of the canvas.

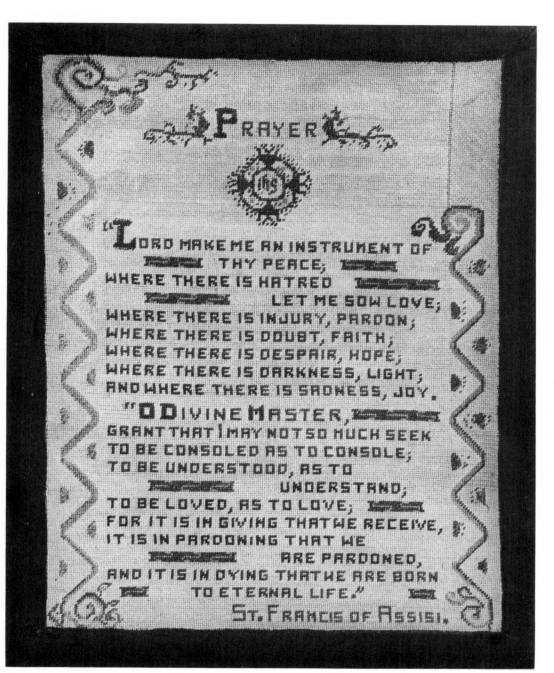

Until six in the morning, we counted out and replanned the whole piece. It was obvious that I would have to start all over again from the very beginning. I wailed, "What about all the work I've done?"

"I guess you can throw it out the window," Jody shrugged, and added, "Unless you want Mr. Loper to think it's just another dumb mistake by another dumb actress."

With this cut rankling, and after all I had been through, I felt downright mean. Then I became suspicious. I began to check the other materials from the shop. Under a warm iron, their "pure silk" curled into pure rayon. The shimmering metallic threads turned pitch black. When I finally closed my weary eyes that morning, the prayer on my lips was not the one spoken by St. Francis. (Somebody must have heard me, because that shop is no longer in business.)

I awakened with fresh resolve. Rechecking the work of the night before, I found Jody was absolutely right—nothing could be salvaged. But I was more determined than ever to do the prayer. This time there would be no mistakes—or if there were, they would be my own. Taking a fresh sheet of graph paper, I proceeded to draw my own version of the design. I laid it out square by square on the page. When it was completed, it pleased me more than anything a shop could do. It's not that it was necessarily a better design than I could buy. It was simply my own, and I felt the pride of creation in it. In this particular case, it was also closer to my original concept! The symbol for Jesus under the word "Prayer" was very ancient, dating back to the first Christian martyrs; the decorative bars and scrollwork came straight from the medieval illumination.

Once the design was established, I needed to procure the materials —the canvas and *pure* silk and gold metallic threads. This was easier said than done; in fact, it developed into quite an odyssey.

To this day there is only a small number of adventurous people who want to do their own work in their own way and who go to the trouble of laying out their own canvases. Nearly fifteen years ago, practically nobody did. The average shops were not set up to sell blank canvas by the yard, nor did they have on hand quantities of wool and silk not already apportioned out to their own prepared designs. I trudged through all the shops listed in the Yellow Pages. It was to no avail: none of them could help. I began to try the department stores, only to meet with the same frustration. I was about to give up, when an assistant buyer in one of the larger stores approached and asked if he could help. I put on the "Sylvia Sidney" look, which one Hollywood director characterized as guaranteed to melt a heart of stone. Then I unconsciously spoke the line I seem to have spoken in just about every movie I have made: "I'm in trouble!"

That director was right. It worked. Strictly against store policy, the assistant buyer wrote me a letter listing all of the store's suppliers.

I hoped the list would be as helpful as it was intended to be. I had wasted a lot of time already, and my deadline for completing the prayer—right after I finished my stock appearances—was not far off. With the letter clutched in one hand and fingers crossed on the other,

I began to make the rounds of the places named. I didn't find exactly what I wanted until halfway down the list, when I came upon the establishments of two remarkable ladies. Both are fortunately still in business (and their addresses are given on page 119).

To meet Miss Kusche I had to journey down to a shabby commercial part of New York. C. R. Meissner Co., her firm, was located in a hotel that had clearly seen better days. It was with some trepidation that I crossed the unprepossessing lobby to her door. What I found inside, however, more than compensated for the long search. It was truly a needleworker's heaven.

Meissner's supplies a great many shops with prepared canvases and the materials to work them. To give you an idea of how delicate their silks and wools are, I need only say that they specialize in needlepoint adaptations of eighteenth-century French masters such as Watteau and Fragonard, and of the pastry-like confections of the nineteenth-century Viennese.

The other lady I found, to whom I am equally indebted, is Miss Joan Toggitt. Her offices in the bustling heart of the city could not be more different from Meissner's. Miss Toggitt sells packaged needlepoint and embroidery, as well as the best books on these crafts. She also keeps a big stock of beautiful wools and silks and the finest canvases imaginable. Although she does not completely eschew *fin-de-siècle* patterns, Miss Toggitt's approach to needlepoint is much less traditional than Meissner's. Perhaps it is because of her contemporary approach that she has always been so gratifyingly encouraging about my work.

Although Meissner normally deals in sizable quantities, and Miss Toggitt's mail-order business is large and demanding, neither of the two ladies hesitated to help me with the small amounts I needed, and both have remained helpful through all the years since.

My ventures among the thread merchants had at last proved successful. Well-provided with blank canvas and yarns, I was actually ready to start work on the prayer. The Misses Kusche and Toggitt gave me no instructions on how to proceed. This I had to learn through many trials and errors and the application of a little common sense.

Obviously, the first step was to transfer my design from the graph paper to the canvas. I cut out and hemmed the canvas, pinned it in place over the drawing, and traced the main outlines of the design. When it came to the lettering, I counted carefully. One line on the graph paper is the equivalent of one mesh on the canvas. So, for the vertical lines in the letters that ran through six squares on the graph paper, I took my magnifying glass and marked off exactly six threads on the canvas. (If you get a good magnifying glass, it will save you a lot of eyestrain. My eyesight seems to have improved since I took up needlepoint. It has the same beneficial results as doing optical exercises. It should go without saying, of course, that a good light is absolutely essential.)

And so I continued, marking off vertically and horizontally the same number of threads on the canvas as were indicated on the graph-paper

sketch. I worked very carefully on the lines of the fanciful scrollwork as well as on the letters of the words, and I was able to make the tracing without a mistake. I cannot stress strongly enough the precision with which the tracing should be done. I have found that needlepoint has a strangely transparent quality. The shadow of any mistake in the inking of a canvas seems to show through even the heaviest yarns in the finished piece.

With the design now drawn on the canvas, I was ready to begin the actual stitchery. At this point, let me interject another suggestion —one that should pose no problem for anybody. Your fingernails should be in perfect condition when you do needlepoint, especially when you are working with silk, because it catches and frays so easily. A rough edge or hangnail can cause a disaster, so have a manicure. (While you are at it, you might as well have your hair done! There is nothing that makes time spent under the dryer go more pleasantly or swiftly than doing needlepoint. It is even better than reading old movie magazines!) Your hands should also be clean—nothing soils so easily as light-colored yarns and silks. I was using a beige silk for the background of the prayer, to create the effect of old parchment, and I made it a point to wash my hands each time I picked up my needle.

I worked feverishly on the prayer all summer, against the deadline of my trip. During rehearsals, before performances, during performances, and after performances, I stitched away. In *Angel Street* I even managed to get a little done on stage. I was playing a Victorian wife; what could be more natural than that she should be doing needlepoint?

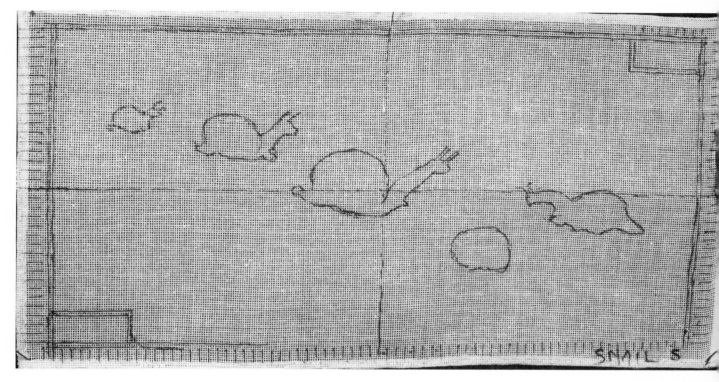

Art and life got mixed up in another way, too. In the play my husband was trying to drive me mad. One of his ploys was to make me believe I couldn't recall where I had put things. Offstage, I found myself living a parallel role. When I returned to my dressing room after each final curtain, my workbasket was never where I distinctly remembered leaving it. Fortunately, the stage manager solved the mystery. A very eager young apprentice actress, who doubled as my dresser (the person who helps one make costume changes), had some exalted notions about the glamour of backstage life. She was hiding my needlepoint, because she thought the canvas, with all those straggling strands of yarn, didn't present the right image of a star to visitors.

Despite all the mishaps, the prayer progressed. I learned a great many things in the course of doing this first original piece. Not the least of them was how to handle metallic thread. At first, the results were distinctly disappointing to me. The gold bars and scrollwork didn't have the bounce and iridescence I sought. They were lackluster, when the whole purpose of using metallic thread was that they glow with life.

With a tweezers, I carefully pulled out all of the gold threads. I didn't know what to to, but because of the pressure of time, I did not dare to stop work completely. For the moment, I simply stitched in with yellow silk the areas where the gold should be, and plowed on. When everything else was finished, I still was undecided about what to do with the metallic thread. I studied the yellow stitchery. It didn't have the kick I wanted, but it did have more life than the gold.

When you cut out the canvas for a piece, leave at least two inches extra on each side, so that there will be a one-and-a-half inch margin after hemming. To transfer the design from graph paper to canvas, the main outlines of the drawing are traced. A good way to do this is to tape the canvas over the graph paper on a window; you can also use heavy carbon paper and a hard, sharp pencil. There is no such thing as a true curve in needlepoint, of course; everything is translated into vertical and horizontal. Trace diagonal lines carefully so they fall exactly where the threads intersect (at the corners of the meshes). Pencil may be used for the first, rough marking, but it rubs off quickly, so you must go over it with indelible ink. And if you apply tints to the canvas to indicate color, be absolutely certain they are colorfast. If a single color runs when the canvas is blocked, the work will be completely ruined. Finally, before you begin to stitch, draw a vertical and a horizontal line through the center of the canvas from edge to edge (use several lines for large pieces). When the canvas is blocked, these lines will be your guides.

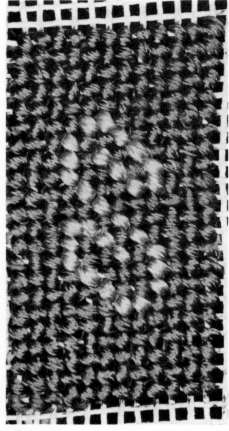

An idea suddenly occurred to me. The yellow had the life, the gold the bright metallic quality. What if I stitched over the yellow with the gold, using the color as a lining under the metal? I had nothing to lose but the extra labor, and so much of that already had been expended on the prayer that a little more could not hurt. And it worked! The metal glowed with life: the effect was exactly what I had imagined.

I finished the prayer just in time to start preparing for my trip to Hollywood, and I was really very proud of it. It possessed exactly the antique feeling that I had envisioned from the day I first saw the medieval manuscript page at the Morgan Library.

All that remained was to block the canvas. I rinsed it in lukewarm water, rolled it in a towel, and tacked it on a board to dry. When that was done, the problem of framing it faced me. I had no idea where Don Loper would hang it, or even in what style his house would be furnished. So I decided that Don could frame it any way that pleased him; but I wanted to do the matting myself. The color of the mat had to pick up the deep reds in the work. Don unwittingly provided the fabric for it. Some years earlier he had designed a perfectly spectacular gown for me, in a timeless Edwardian style. It was made of a rich shade of garnet silk velvet and taffeta; on one side, at the hip, a great pouf broke and ended in a flowing train. This was perfect for great balls but rather cumbersome for at-homes. I had reached a time in my life when the occasions for ballgowns were limited—I could certainly dispense with part of the train. I cut off enough to miter and sew to the prayer.

The moment I arrived in Hollywood, Don and I went to work on fittings for my costumes. I carried the prayer around in a plain paper bag, not knowing how to give it to him and too shy to make any great ceremony of the presentation. One day, after a fitting session, he invited me to Romanoff's for a drink. I made up my mind to use the occasion. Romanoff's was a restaurant that catered to Hollywood's royalty. The beat-up paper bag I casually pushed across the table was probably the first of its kind ever seen in the regal establishment.

Don was both delighted and moved by what it held. I had found the right gift, and all the effort had been worthwhile. The prayer now hangs in Don's library, where it looks very fine indeed. And so, an idea born in Mr. Morgan's library traveled three thousand miles across a continent to find a congenial home in Mr. Loper's.

The prayer was the start of many things for me. Above all, since that time, I have always marked my canvases myself. Jody's solution— the graph paper—was what liberated me from dependence on prepared, store-designed canvases.

At first, all I did was copy pictures that caught my fancy. I simply

A rule of thumb for working with metallic thread, whether gold or silver, is always to understitch it with silk. The intensity and quality of the metallic shimmer depend completely upon the tone of the thread underneath. Bright golden yellow understitching gives an overlay of gold thread a glaring, brassy brilliance. Silk shaded down towards mustard yellow tends to age and tarnish the gold, lending it a muted, coppery character. With silver thread, white understitching gives the brightness of newly polished sterling, while shading down through the grays dulls the effect to a pewter.

traced them onto graph paper, counted the squares, and knew precisely the number of meshes needed to duplicate them on canvas. This was easy when the pictures were large enough to reproduce in the same size on canvas. Enlarging small ones presented a problem in the beginning, but the solution proved simple. For very little money— a small fraction of what it costs to have a canvas designed for you— you can have a picture photostated to the exact size you want to trace on your canvas. Any photography shop will do it. More important than the amount of money that you save by marking your own canvas, I think you will find the same satisfaction I feel in doing a piece from scratch all by myself.

When I became daring enough to do original designs, I followed the same procedure. I do all of my sketching and coloring on graph paper. When I am completely happy with the look of the design, I trace it onto the canvas. The graph-paper sketch, like the pictures I copied before, serves as my point of reference for color.

With every canvas I was learning something—a technique, a way of

Blocking a canvas is done very simply by washing it in soap and lukewarm water. Any soap suitable for delicate fabrics (never a detergent) or one of the foams made for cleaning upholstery can be used. (Rabbit glue, available in art-supply stores, may be applied to very delicate pieces before washing, but the process is very messy and not essential.) Rinse the canvas thoroughly and roll it in a Turkish towel. While it is still damp, stretch it and tack it to a board with pushpins or nails. Boards marked in inches and half-inches can be purchased or made (cork is a good surface to use). It is very important to stretch the canvas quite square by aligning the vertical and horizontal center lines, and the dimensions should be checked against the original measurements of the canvas. Let the piece dry completely. Finally, if it is likely to get hard wear, it may be Scotch-guarded.

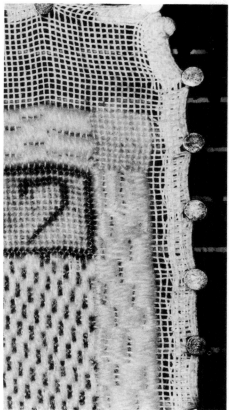

TENT STITCH

see page 84

STRAIGHT GOBELIN STITCH

see page 96

dealing with materials, a way of achieving an effect I desired. For example, there were the roses.

Don Loper is one of the most thoughtful men I know. He never forgets a birthday or anniversary, and he has always said that no matter how bad times are, one can always afford to remember a special occasion with one white rose. It is a lovely sentiment, and it inspired the designs for two gifts I made for Christmas, 1962. I did one white rose for Don and another for his partner and my friend, Charles Northrup. I knew Don would like white on white; for Charles I decided on a blue background—he had shown me a sample of blue velvet with which he intended to cover a sofa in his home.

Needlepointing a white rose on a white background posed a new problem for me. A few surrounding leaves would help to give the flower a little definition, but how was I to suggest the volume and depth of the blossom? First I thought of using different stitchery. But I discarded the idea, because it would provide only a textural distinction rather than one intrinsic to the flower. Then I approached the problem from a painter's point of view. I took out my pad of graph paper and did a watercolor sketch. The shading came to me naturally. The petals were highlighted in the softest of greens, vaguely echoing the leaves, and the palest of yellows. I chose Tent Stitch for its classic simplicity. Because of the essential whiteness, however, I wanted a textural border that would define the edges of the hanging clearly, so I executed it in Straight Gobelin.

There was no difficulty in defining the form of the second rose, because of the blue background. I again used Tent Stitch on penelope canvas. I wanted this rose to be different from the other, however, so I designed it with a stalk. In addition, I thought it would be fun to work into the background all of Charles' many nicknames—Chuckle, Chuck, Charlie, Cherles. I toyed with several ideas before it came to

me that, instead of using a different color or stitch, I might use a different material. I stitched the names into the blue wool background in exactly the same shade of blue silk. The result was just right. Hold the pillow in a direct light, and the names completely disappear into the background. Angle the pillow or move the light, and the sheen of the silk reflects the light so the names emerge. By thinking with my needle, I had stumbled upon a nice blend of playfulness and simple design.

Art training in creating original designs is by no means an absolute requirement. Even a great natural talent is not called for: for instance, the extent of my own abilities as an artist can be summed up best by the all-inclusive general description of Sunday painter. I can freely admit that I have rarely been struck by blazing inspiration in the manner of the great painters and sculptors. It has been enough to know that what I make will be something somebody will love. I once read that Salvador Dali loved hippopotamuses, and so I did a hippo in needlepoint. I didn't expect that Dali would ever see it—this was not even a consideration. It was sufficient to know that somebody loved a hippopotamus—somebody, that is, besides another hippopotamus!

Starting with the prayer, each new piece of needlepoint became a challenge. I constantly asked myself "What if . . . ?" and allowed my needle to find the answer. There was no need for formal instruction or vast research. After I learned the rudiments of needlepoint, I always made the materials work for me instead of forcing me to work for them. That is the only real secret behind anything I may have accomplished in my work.

I want to demonstrate that, within the limitations of needle, canvas, and yarn, needlepoint can be marvelously flexible. It is during the moments when you "doodle" with a needle that you can stumble upon the greatest riches.

2. Waste Not, Want Not—A Love Story

For a long while I was very contented with the series of flowers, bumblebees, four-leaf clovers, and such, on which I worked after the St. Francis prayer. In the beginning the mere fact that I was doing my own designs on canvas was enough to keep me satisfied. After that, small experiments with new stitches and different gauges of canvas whetted my interest. But finally the day came when I had to admit that there was a repetitious quality to what I was doing. The sense of challenge was being replaced by a mere mechanical proficiency. I needed a stimulus—some new challenge.

A tin of pâté de foie gras and a can of soup accidentally provided it. In 1960 there was an enormous exhibition of French products at the New York Coliseum. I was first in line the day after the show opened: not even De Gaulle has ever been able to dampen my affection for the food of his country. Imagine being able to get all the genuine petite marmite and truffled pâté you want without having to renew either your passport or your smallpox inoculation!

My arms were loaded down with wonderful provisions when I came upon a display that was to change my entire direction in needlepoint. The venerable looms of the Gobelin and Aubusson factories, on which rugs and tapestries were made for the French royal family from the middle of the sixteenth century right down to the last Louis, had been revitalized. Still operated by the old techniques, they were being used to make tapestries from designs by some of France's greatest modern painters, including Picasso and Leger. There were also works (a series of astrological signs) by Lurçat, the well-known designer of contemporary tapestries.

I looked at the exciting colors and bold lines of these vivid hangings. It seemed incredible that nobody had done this sort of work in needlepoint. It is true that in loomed tapestry much greater variety of effect is possible. Then again, it seemed to me, one might be able to compensate for the limitations by the fineness of stitchery and delicacy of shading that can be achieved in needlepoint. The idea of doing a modern tapestry in needlepoint became very exciting. And, for some reason, visions of frogs and mushrooms were popping into my head. Perhaps it was the proximity of all that wonderful French food.

The more I thought about it, the more excited I became, and the more I visualized of my new project. I would do a forest scene—not a naturalistic forest, but one akin in feeling to the primitive works of the great painter, Henri Rousseau. I have always adored the manner in which he handled foliage and color.

When I got home, I sat down and began to sketch frogs and mushrooms. As I worked, I discovered that they possessed myriad design qualities. I gradually became aware of shape and hue and texture that

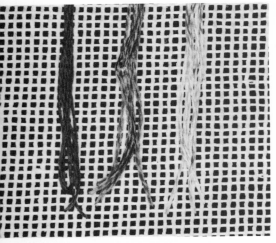

Three shades of silk are blended in a sample done in Tent Stitch on a mono 16. From upper right to lower left, the bands were worked as follows: shade 1; shade 2; shade 3; two strands of shade 3 and two strands of shade 2; shade 2 alone; two strands of shade 2 and two strands of shade 1; shade 1 alone. The blending is more subtle where the shades are mixed together. The trick is not to worry about how the shades show up: a speckled effect brings color to life. For instance, if a little yellow is mixed with several greens, or even one strand of red with three of green, the color will sparkle.

until then had escaped my attention. I decided that I had better check my observations against those of professional artists.

The house began to overflow with all sorts of books and old prints illustrating animals, insects, flowers, and trees. Strangely enough, the most helpful were children's books. To keep a youngster's interest, illustrations have to be bold, simple, explicit, and colorful. These qualities make them especially valuable for the needleworker, because they can easily be traced onto graph paper. Through the years, they have become a great source of inspiration in my work. My subject matter may be a little more sophisticated than that found in the pages of a second-grade reader, but I have always sought the feeling of simplicity and directness that characterizes the best examples of juvenile-book illustration.

After I had made countless preliminary sketches, my concept of the size and composition of the tapestry began to take form. In persuing source materials, I discovered that the frog and mushroom were oriental symbols of good fortune, as were the praying mantis, butterfly, snail, and ladybug. They fitted so perfectly into my vision of the tapestry that I decided to include them all.

I was finally ready to design the piece. It was to be twenty-two by forty-four inches. Graph paper doesn't come in this size, so I pasted several sheets together to make a page large enough to hold the drawing. I was so carried away by the monumental size of the sketch and by the whole project that subtleties of shading and line crept in: these were obviously going to present a problem in execution. To get the various effects demanded by the graph-paper cartoon, I needed to combine very fine stitchery—petit point—with stitches done on a larger mesh. Rather than accommodate my design to the conventional methods I had used hitherto, I decided to experiment with a technique I had never tried before. This was to use a penelope canvas and work on the single threads as well as the double ones. I selected a penelope 10-20, which would give me twenty threads to the inch for the petit point and ten threads to the inch for the other stitchery.

The praying mantis, ladybugs, and frog were the most finely detailed figures; they had to be done in petit point. As I worked on them, I realized that the silk I was using was providing neither the highlighting nor the shading of my design. To achieve the delicacy I desired, I would have to create new colors. So I tried mixing together the colors I had, in various combinations to get the effects I wanted.

It was a very easy process. Wool and silk for needlepoint are composed of several individual strands twisted together. I simply took two or more lengths of different colors, detached from each as many strands as I needed to mix a new shade.

Doing the coloring this way was delightful; and the spectrum that thereby became available greatly broadened the scope of the work. For example, when I couldn't find a commercially made-up shade between a bright orange and a muted yellow, I blended the two together and created it.

To achieve the wispy, fragile feeling of distant vines, I again sepa-

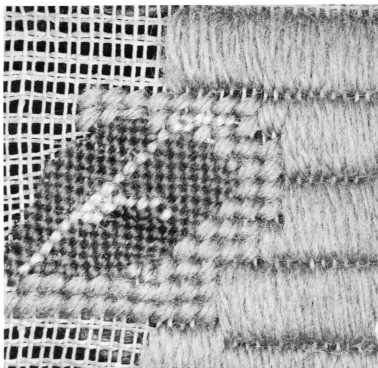

Petit point is needlepoint done on a small-gauge canvas (usually sixteen threads to the inch or more). One method of combining petit point and regular stitchery (gros point) on the same canvas is illustrated above. The first picture shows petit point done with split strands of silk on the separated threads of a penelope canvas. In the following steps, areas of Half-Cross and Gobelin were added on the double threads. Although any stitch may be used for petit point, the most common is Tent Stitch.

rated the threads of the canvas and split the silk, working it in Tent Stitch. For the less detailed objects in the design—the snail, mushroom, and butterfly—I used Half-Cross Stitch on double threads, splitting and mixing strands of silk for delicacy of accent. The larger areas of foliage and the entire background were done in Straight Gobelin, which has a handsome texture and works very quickly—a great advantage in doing backgrounds. To give the background a dynamic quality, I mixed together several shades of beige, and added a few strands of gray. I also found that with Gobelin it is easy to combine silk and wool in the same stitch. The results were very satisfying: the wool gave the area sturdiness, while the silk contributed sparkle.

HALF-CROSS STITCH

see page 83

As long as I have mentioned Gobelin, let me digress for a moment to address needleworkers who are reluctant to use it. Many people have told me that it looks difficult. The appearance is deceiving. If you will try only one row (see the instructions on page 96), you will see how simple it really is. I only suggest that you take the trouble to mark the canvas before starting to stitch. You can then do the stitch automatically, without having to stop to count meshes.

It was impossible for me to devote all my time to working on the tapestry. In addition to an engagement of Tennessee Williams' *Sweet Bird of Youth,* as the Princess, I had promised several smaller pieces to friends as presents. Some of these were for special occasions, such as birthdays, and I couldn't very well put them aside. Deadlines were becoming a daily concern, but I was enjoying myself so thoroughly that it usually didn't even seem like work. One of the nicest things about needlework is that the sense of accomplishment doesn't come only at the completion of a piece. It is present constantly, as the canvas fills up stitch by stitch.

Finally, however, the tapestry was finished (see the frontispiece) and ready to be blocked—it had taken me about six months. I rinsed the canvas, and then discovered that I had no board large enough to stretch it on. In desperation, I tacked it up on a door. One evening, while it was still drying, a friend arrived to take me to a party. I wanted an opinion of my handiwork and showed it to him. He stared at the door and said, "Sylvia, what are you thinking of? It looks like the entrance to a Chinese opium den." It was not exactly the reaction I was hoping for. But it was comforting to see that at least he recognized the oriental influence.

The gentleman was Morton DaCosta—or Teak, as he is affectionately known to his friends. He was the brilliant director of both the Broadway and motion-picture versions of *Auntie Mame* and *The Music Man,* and many other shows. In my time, like every actress, I have had differences of opinion with directors. But Teak is the only one I ever put in a sick bed—and he never even directed me. It was because of a piece of needlework, and I think the story might prove a valuable lesson in the necessity for restraint among novice needleworkers.

On the way to the party, I told Teak all about the needlepoint I had been doing. He became very enthusiastic. His doctor had recently told him he should find a pastime that would help him relax after the ten-

sions of his work. He was so impressed with the tapestry that he decided to follow his doctor's advice and take up needlepoint himself. Since he had just moved into a new apartment, and had a set of dining room chairs that needed re-covering, I encouraged him to start where I had started—with the chairs. I recommended some good books of instruction and a shop where he could get his materials and additional help, if he wanted it.

A few weeks later I called to find out how he was getting on. His secretary told me that he couldn't come to the phone. He was confined to his bed; it was doctor's orders. When I asked what was wrong, she responded hesitantly, "Well—you see—he hurt himself doing needlepoint."

I had not taken into account the determination of a man who had risen to the top of one of the world's most exacting professions. He assimilated the instructions, gathered his materials, and sat down in a large chair to set to work. He literally did not stir out of the chair for two days. Even his meals were brought to him on a tray. When he finally finished the first canvas and got up, he keeled over with acute vertigo. Consequently, the doctor had ordered him to remain flat on his back in a darkened room for a week. Although the memory must pain him every time he uses them, Teak can take some consolation in the fact that the chairs, which he finished—at a sensible pace—upon recovery, did turn out very handsomely.

Teak's mishap was the only unfortunate thing ever to happen in connection with the tapestry. The good-luck symbols certainly worked for me. I exhibited the tapestry in needlepoint shows at the New Hope (Pennsylvania) Historical Society and the Illinois Festival of Art, and it was greatly admired. It was the subject of a picture story in *Designer International* and was reproduced in color on the cover of the magazine. The photographer was my son, Jody.

Even the leftover wool and silk found a happy use. My tendency is to buy too much yarn, usually because I fall in love with the colors. This is not so extravagant as you might think: the materials are not expensive, and the leftovers can always be used in another piece. Pinks, greens, and oranges will certainly find their future place as flowers; any hues can be utilized in an infinite variety of combinations in an overall Bargello design. (By the way, what I have already said about Gobelin is also true of Bargello. If you will try one line, you will see how easy it is to achieve the beautiful effects of the stitch.) As a matter of fact, I always keep a piece of hemmed odd-sized canvas available and work on it with scraps for relaxation. Out of these unconventional shapes come pillows (such as the one shown on page 27), coasters, hairbands, belts, decorative patch-pockets, purses, book covers, and many other fast-working gifts.

The extra yarns from the tapestry became a present for my close friend Jan Miner. Even if you have never seen her onstage, you would probably recognize her familiar voice and face from television commercials for everything from Goodman's noodles to Palmolive soap, or from her long stint as a very weepy lady in the serial program, *Edge of Night*.

BARGELLO STITCH

see page 109

When Jan saw the tapestry, she was very flattering in her admiration. Her greatest praise was reserved for the colors. I knew she would have liked a similar piece for herself, but I simply could not face the prospect of doing another canvas that large so soon. I decided to surprise her with some cushions, which I would make from the leftover wool.

I cut two pieces of canvas and hemmed them to the dimensions of the pillows. Starting with Jan's initials in one corner, I improvised the entire abstract design, using a combination of Straight Gobelin and Half-Cross Stitch.

When I brought Jan the finished work (see page 27), she looked at it and said, "You're crazy!" I was taken aback. She continued, "Have you got something against money?" I was more confused than ever. Then she explained what she meant.

"Instead of giving your work away," she suggested, "why don't you sell it? I'd like you to make some things for me to give as Christmas presents. But I won't ask unless you let me pay for them." And then and there she took out her checkbook and gave me my first order. This was *really* inspiring!

What Jan wanted was a series of pillows, wallets, and cosmetic cases that had on them the initials and astrological signs of the people for whom they were intended. I was delighted, because it gave me the opportunity I wanted. Ever since I first saw the Lurçat tapestries at the Coliseum show, the idea of working the signs of the Zodiac had been in the back of my mind. Now that I had a commission, I did some research and learned that a color, flower, and gem were associated with each of the signs. This information made the project even more interesting, because it broadened the scope of what could legitimately be included in the designs.

One of the pieces I particularly enjoyed doing was a pillow for the actress Nancy Walker, her composer husband, David Craig, and their daughter, Miranda. I wanted it to have a playful, almost carnival quality that would be right for an inspired clown like Nancy. After discarding several sketches, I arrived at the design—a series of gaily colored balloons (see page 27). On each of three balloons I put the initial of one member of the Craig household, and just in front of each of these balloons was another containing the sign of the Zodiac under which that person was born. The initials and symbols were worked in pale blue silk; the balloons and background were in wool. The entire cushion was executed in Tent Stitch.

I later did another, amusing pillow for the Craigs (see page 80). David, talking one day of his work as a leading coach of singers and actors, uttered fervently the prayer, "O Lord, give me a bastard with talent!"

We all laughed, and Nancy immediately commissioned me to do it in needlepoint. I worked it in white letters decorated with gold on a black background, using Half-Cross and Tent Stitch on a penelope canvas.

I combined an astrological sign with one of the good-luck symbols from the tapestry to decorate another piece I made as a special present. It was for Ben Strobach, the young man who served as advance man when I did a summer tour of *Anniversary Waltz*, and as stage manager when I did the national tour in *Auntie Mame*. The stage manager is the man who makes an actress' life bearable and, sometimes, unbearable—he is responsible for seeing that everything from the actress herself to her costumes and props is exactly where it should be, when it should be. He sees that when you reach for cigarettes in a box, they are there, and that when you expect an actor to make his entrance, he does. In a show as complicated and with as many quick costume changes as *Mame*, the stage manager is especially indispensable. I decided to show my gratitude to Ben by doing a vest in needlepoint for him.

I settled on a plain brown-gray for the background and chose as the design elements Ben's initials, which I did in gold metallic thread, a tiny red ladybug for luck, a yellow lion for Ben's astrological sign, and a green snake for me. ("Snakie" was the nickname the cast gave me during the tour. No matter what it may sound like, I insist they meant it affectionately.) I did the entire vest in silk, using Tent Stitch on a mono 20.

When the canvases were finished, I showed them to Ben. As I have said, the figures were very small and, I thought, conservative. Unfortunately, Ben was even more conservative. He said, "Snakie, it's beautiful—but where would I wear a silk vest?"

I console myself now with the knowledge that I was really ahead of my time. In these days of the male peacock, a silk vest would be a wonderful gift.

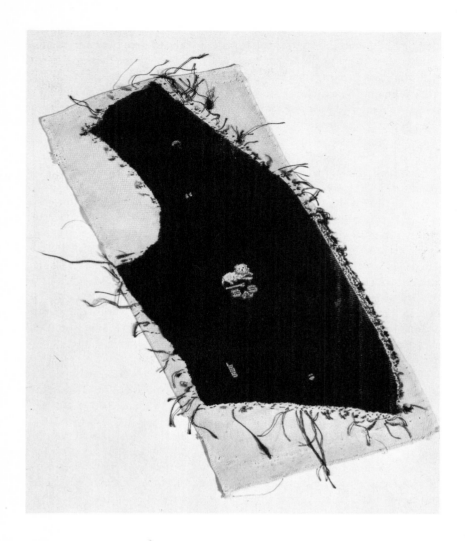

Despite Ben's protests, I was determined that he have the vest, so I turned my attention to getting it made up. I had no idea what a problem it would be. At those places where the work could be done, the prices were exorbitant; most places would not do it at any price. Even Ben's tailor turned us down. We had really reached an impasse when Ben said wistfully, "If only you'd made a cushion. I mean—they're so practical. Even when it's too hot to wear a vest, you can always use a cushion."

So I solved the problem by cutting down the panels, rehemming them, and making pillows. Ben had his present, and we were both delighted.

Another piece based on the astrological symbols taught me a lesson of a different kind. One day Jan Miner rushed in to see me in a state of great excitement. She blurted out, "I'm in love. And he's a crab." I was terribly sympathetic. I said I knew exactly what she was going through—I had once been in love with one myself.

Jan interrupted my condolences with a withering glance. "Sylvia. Cancer. The crab. His astrological sign! I want to give him one of your pillows as a present. With his sign on it. It's got to be the most beautiful thing you've ever made."

How in the world can a crab look beautiful? I thought about it for a while. It finally occurred to me that the only time the creature could ever remotely approach good looks is when it first emerges from the sea, still sparkling with drops of water. It was that moment I would have to capture in needlepoint.

It was all worked in wool and silk in a combination of straight Tent Stitch and Diagonal Tent Stitch. Black and garnet red are the colors associated with the sign of the Crab, so I used them in the border. This was a continuous pattern of the monogram of Richard Merrell, the gifted set designer for whom the pillow was intended. The repeated motif created the effect of a Greek key rather than a series of letters. The body of the crab was executed in tones of blue and green, to which I added touches of other colors in an unsuccessful attempt to create the quality of iridescence. As a last resort, I decided to see what would happen if I tried some accents of silk. I repeated the overstitching procedure I used when I worked with metallic thread, only this time with silk over wool. Again my experiment worked! The crab did indeed look as if it had just rolled out of the surf into the sun.

The following year, while I was appearing on Broadway in the comedy, *Enter Laughing,* I received an excited call from my friend Jan, who announced that she and Dick Merrell were going to get married. "It's going to be a double-ring ceremony," she told me. "The date's all set. May 5th. And, darling, we'd both just love it if you'd make the ring pillow."

The problem that confronted me in this project was finding the right design. Knowing the couple's taste, I didn't want to do anything too old fashioned. At the same time, the Wedding March is not exactly a pop hit, and a very modern design would also be wrong. This pillow had a specific purpose. The design had to express it appropriately.

I found the answer in an old Pennsylvania Dutch drawing of a double love knot, which represented the ring ceremony perfectly. I combined the knot with the couple's initials, adapting a medieval script to impart a feeling of the timelessness of the marriage rites. Finally, between the ends of the last tie of the knot I placed the wedding date (see page 27).

White silk thread was an absolute requirement for the background of the pillow; for the details of the design I chose a combination of Dick and Jan's favorite colors, mustardy yellows and greens. I did the entire piece in Straight Gobelin, varying the number of meshes over which the stitches were done. Gobelin not only has a beautiful texture but also, as I have said, can be worked quickly. It is my favorite stitch when I am pressed for time, and the wedding date was a compelling deadline.

It was interesting for me to observe that certain constants were developing in my attitude towards my work. I am sure that many other

needleworkers have shared them. First and foremost, a piece does not have to be complex or difficult to do to be satisfying. It has only to give pleasure to the person for whom it is intended—the more he or she loves it, the more satisfaction it gives me.

Second, needlepoint is never a chore for me. Even when I am working against a deadline or have encountered a snag so irritating that I think I will lose my mind, I still enjoy the work.

Finally, I discovered how frugal I am. I hate to waste anything I have done. I will go to any lengths—experiment with seemingly formidable techniques, even try my hand at inventing new methods—rather than abandon a piece.

These attitudes were leading me in many new directions, but I did not realize that anything unusual was happening. What I was doing was the only thing I knew how to do. Right or wrong, I simply approached needlepoint in the same way I have approached everything else I have ever tried—from a strictly personal point of view.

3. Some People Like Monkeys, Some People Like Turtles, and Some Go to Princeton

Recently, Dorothy Rodgers, Russell Lynes, Joan Fontaine, and I were interviewed on television by Aline Saarinen, NBC's art critic. The subject was needlepoint, and we all had brought samples of our work. As befits a lady who is not only a renowned hostess as the wife of the distinguished composer, Richard Rodgers, but also a successful interior decorator, Mrs. Rodgers exhibited a lovely rug. Mr. Lynes, a social commentator and very well-dressed gentleman, showed a vest. Miss Fontaine displayed some slippers and pillows that were as pretty and graceful as she herself is. Then I held up my designs: an owl, a monkey, and a turtle. Mrs. Saarinen asked, "Why all the animals?"

"They sell!" I exclaimed, without thinking. Realizing that this conveyed a meaning I had not intended, I went on to explain. "Well, what's the use of doing all this work if it doesn't please somebody? I do animals because people seem to like them."

I had decided to take Jan Miner's advice to sell some of my work. To my astonishment, people did express interest in buying it, and orders started to come in immediately. Animals were among the subjects most requested, and they naturally began to occupy a great part of my thoughts and efforts.

In doing an animal, my starting point is always the eyes. This is where the expression is to be found. Animals are not unlike film actors in this respect. In fact, some actors have been very conscious of it. The famous critic, George Jean Nathan, once asked Lillian Gish how she got such great expression into her eyes. Miss Gish replied, "I always look at dogs and study them very closely. Everything they feel is conveyed by their eyes."

Once the manner in which the eyes are to be handled is established, the rest of the design generally falls into place. There are a number of qualities that make animals interesting subjects. They are individuals: even members of the same species are really very different in carriage, personality, and appearance. Two elegant giraffes possess characteristics as distinctive as two elegant fashion models. I would no more mistake one for the other than I would Twiggy for Suzy Parker.

The more needlepoint I did, the more inventive I had to become in the execution of each piece. I wanted my work to have a look that would make it different from that of other needleworkers. This involved using techniques that others might not attempt or combining ordinary methods and materials in my own way. It was not as difficult as it might sound. For the most part it arose quite naturally out of my good old fuss and fumble. Not one of the pieces I have ever made is

beyond the capability of anybody who has ever put needle to canvas.

What happened on a very early commission demonstrates what I mean perfectly. Mrs. Harcourt Amory was one of my first and greatest boosters. She ordered a pillow for Christmas of 1964. The design was to be two frogs sitting on toadstools (see page 57). I decided that a penelope canvas would best suit the needs of the piece. I could separate the threads and do the bodies of the frogs and the toadstools in petit Gobelin with split and mixed strands of silk. Although the work went fairly rapidly, I knew that I would only just have it finished in time for the holiday. Then came disaster! The hot red background, which had looked perfectly fine in my graph-paper sketch, looked perfectly awful in the canvas stitchery. It completely overwhelmed the delicate little toadstools and frogs. My first impulse was to throw out the entire piece and start all over again. But this not only went against my frugal nature; it also meant that Mrs. Amory would not have her pillow for Christmas. I had to find a way to salvage at least part of the piece.

There was nothing wrong with the figures, so I decided to rip out the entire background, thinking I would redo it from scratch. I worked into the morning. I didn't know it at the time, but there would be many more sleepless nights in the years to follow. It seems to me that I have had to spend more nights walking the floor with a sick piece of needlepoint than I ever had to with my child.

The tedious job of ripping out the stitches proved a futile one. It was much too wearing on the canvas: when I was finished, the threads were not strong enough to stitch over again. I wasn't certain what to try next. Still hoping I could find a way to save the figures, I cut around them, leaving a very broad border. I ruled out appliquéing them to a fresh canvas because the stitched edges would be too lumpy for a delicate pillow. The only thing that seemed possible was somehow to weave them in.

I carefully frayed away the border right up to the edges of the figures, leaving strands that were long enough to thread through a needle. Then I sewed each individual thread into the new canvas behind the figures. I either knotted the threads in the back or wove them through the canvas so carefully that the figures were undisturbed. It was a painstaking and slow process, but it worked. In addition to getting me out of a very difficult situation, it also gave me another opportunity. I found, in placing the figures on the new canvas, that I could put them in a different and more pleasing arrangement. I later learned that what I had dreamed up out of desperation was a very old technique, seldom if ever used anymore.

The new background color I selected was one that was far more sympathetic to the little frogs and toadstools. It was a muted brownish-green, which I executed in Diagonal Tent Stitch. To give the pillow a frame with some bounce, I bordered it with Old Florentine Stitch in pale beige.

Perhaps it was the idea that the frogs and I now shared a secret that made me want to put a mischievous gleam in their eyes. This was ac-

OLD FLORENTINE STITCH

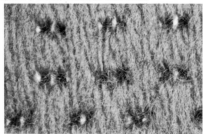

see page 101

complished merely by sewing black caviar beads into them. I used a beading needle and silk thread and stitched them on in the ordinary way. To be sure they were firmly attached, I was careful to sew through both canvases.

Very few people use beads in needlepoint, and I, for one, have always thought it a shame. Years ago they often formed part of needlepoint designs. I have two very old footstools in which they are not sewn on but woven right into the body of the work. This would probably prove a time-consuming and cumbersome job, but there is no reason why beads cannot be stitched on for accents and special effects such as eyes or drops of dew on a flower petal. The result can be attractive as well as amusing.

Once I was certain of the success of the two-canvas technique, I couldn't wait to try it again. This time I wanted to make it a definite element of the design scheme right from the first sketch. I postponed starting, however, because of a problem that recurs with almost every new piece I do.

After I have sketched and painted the design on graph paper and then carefully traced the outline onto the canvas, I find myself becoming apprehensive. I select the colors and threads I want. The actual materials generally delight me, but the sense of apprehension increases. Invariably I find myself putting off that weighty moment when I must actually make the first stitch. I pace around, staring at the sketch and the canvas and the threads and thinking they will never come together into a unified whole. The conviction grows that I cannot remember how to do the stitches I want to use. Naturally, this means I have to get down all my instruction books; then, naturally, I have to put them back. My excuses for procrastination are unlimited.

I suppose that the first stitch is a little bit like an opening night. You know your lines, you know exactly what you have to do, you have been very well rehearsed, but it is still absolute agony to take that first step onto the stage.

Fortunately, Mrs. Amory came to my rescue, as someone or something always does. She was so pleased with the frogs that she wanted another pillow in the same style. That gave me an objective, and a deadline. I am compulsive about the obligation to meet deadlines. This, probably, is what makes me face the terror of merely putting one foot in front of the other to get on the stage on opening night.

My idea for Mrs. Amory's second pillow was a little more fanciful than for the first. Two things of which I am extremely fond are the shape of giraffes and the taste of wild strawberries. It seemed natural to me that a giraffe would love strawberries, too. The problem was that, because of the giraffe's height, he probably never had seen a strawberry, much less tasted one. So I decided to bring them together. All I needed to do was rearrange nature a little. It is a task much more painlessly accomplished with a needle than some of the other methods people have tried through the ages. I simply made the berries so large that the giraffe couldn't possibly miss them.

Instead of fitting the giraffe into the normal square of a pillow, I

turned the canvas on the bias and worked it as a diamond, making the shape serve the design. This enabled me to follow the lines of the body of the animal, foreshorten the legs, and give much greater prominence to the strawberries (see page 60).

The colors I chose for this design contrasted, but didn't clash, with those in the first pillow. To link the two, I made the entire background the same pale beige as the Old Florentine frame around the frogs, only here done in Brick Stitch. This is a stitch that, like Gobelin, works fast and covers a large area handsomely.

The main canvas, on which I worked the giraffe and the background, was a mono 16. I did the body of the animal in split wool, the hooves and eyes in silk, so they would have luster. To give the eyes added expression and brightness, I inserted blue and black beads and a tiny simulated pearl with my beading needle. The strawberries were done on a mono 30, which I then wove into the larger canvas. For the tiny seeds, I sewed on steel-cut beads.

Among the canvases I worked on in this period was a large frog hopping through swampy mud. I was curious about how much variety could be obtained in a piece executed completely in Tent Stitch. I used a penelope 11-22 canvas. The body of the frog was done in silk, the eyes and feet on separated threads. To give the figure a little more

BRICK STITCH

see page 100

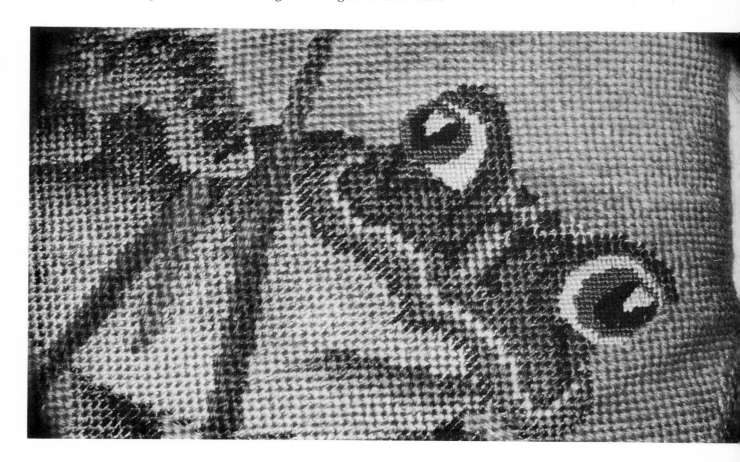

1

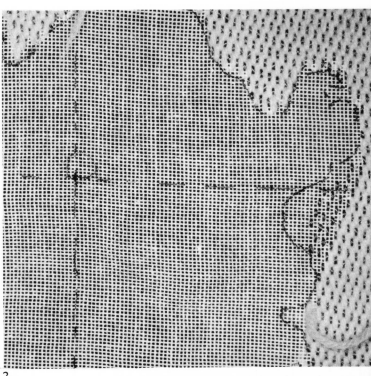

2

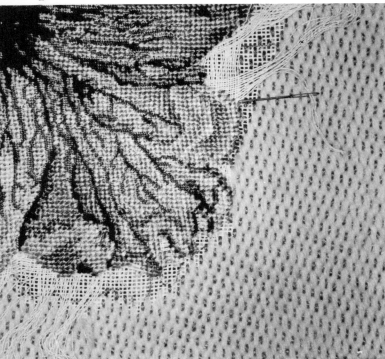

5

6

This sequence of pictures illustrates the procedure for inserting one canvas into another.

1. The design is laid out on graph-paper. It is then traced on to two canvases—the smaller one that is to be inserted and the larger, into which it is to be inserted.

2. On the larger canvas, the background stitch is done very nearly to the edge of the traced outline of the insert.

3. After the piece to be inserted is completed, the border is ravelled to the edge of the stitchery. Remember to leave long enough strands to thread a needle.

4. Pin the insert to where it is to be positioned in the background.

5. Thread the needle with the ravelled strands of smaller canvas. Sew it into larger canvas.

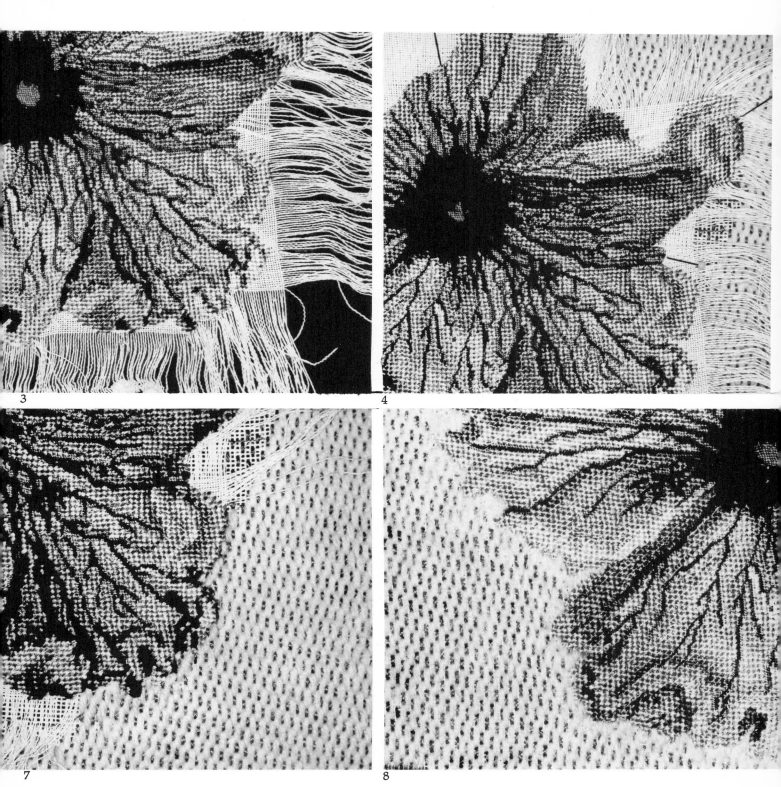

3

4

7

8

6. At back of larger canvas, either knot off the strands **or** weave them back into the smaller canvas, being careful not to disturb the design.

7. Continue this all the way around the insert until all of the strands have been sewn in.

8. Finally, stitch in bits of the uncompleted larger canvas to the edge of the insertion. It is very important to do

these stitches over the remaining exposed threads of the insert (here, the ones between the petals of the flower).

The procedure is the same whether you use two or three canvases. On page 44 you can see the stages in a three-canvas work. The center of the black-eyed Susan is on a fine-mesh canvas; the petals are on a medium gauge; and the background is on a large-mesh piece.

definition against the background, I outlined it in black, using an ordinary backstitch. Then I thought the leaves needed some sparkle, so I overstitched the wool with silk. Finally, I had noticed that using only one color wool for a large area done in Tent Stitch could be monotonous, so I did the background in tones shading from pale beige to light brown.

Everyone has heard of the old school tie. Mr. Dean Mathey went it one better when he commissioned me to do an old school pillow (see page 60). Mr. Mathey comes from a long and distinguished line of Princetonians, and he wanted my design to commemorate both the year of the university's founding and the year of its greatest football victories. Naturally, a tiger—Princeton's mascot—had to dominate the design.

I didn't think the tiger should be ferocious; after all, he had already defeated his opponents. Instead, I tried to make him playful, rather like a toy or cartoon animal, to express some of the spirit of undergraduate days. This is why his enormously long tail is wagging right out of the picture into the frame at the top, and with one paw he is triumphantly pushing the football down into the frame at the bottom. I believe he must be thinking that another season with such a string of victories is not likely to come along soon again, because the poor creature looks just a little worried.

The whole pillow was done on one canvas, a penelope 10-20. I separated the threads and did the figure of the tiger and the football in petit point. The background is Tent Stitch; the border, diagonal Scotch

Stitch. The football gave me almost as much trouble as it did Princeton's opponents. No matter what I did, it reminded me of a half-eaten brown casaba melon, and I was trying to honor the school's athletic prowess, not its dining clubs. The dates on the ball actually served as camouflage. Stitching the numbers was a bit of a problem, but I finally solved it by simply embroidering them over the petit point.

I continued to explore new ways in needlepoint. I felt rather like Columbus: I was fairly certain there was something to be discovered on the other side, but I was not at all certain what it was. As I recall how and why each piece was done in a particular way, I realize that the "why" was often the reason for the result.

Another project I worked on was a pair of jungle pillows (see pages 40-41). One showed a leopard sprawled on the branch of a tree; the other a monkey perching on what might be another branch of the same tree. I used exactly the same technique for both. They were done on penelope canvas, and I separated the threads and used petit point for the bodies, working them in split wool and silk. I did the backgrounds in the same shades of red and yellow, using Half-Cross Stitch on toned Tramé. Tramé is a series of long stitches executed in either silk or split wool done on the canvas as a backing; the regular stitches are worked over it. It functions in roughly the same way for needlepoint as underpainting for an oil painting. It gives the work greater body and so is especially valuable when you are using the Half-Cross

SCOTCH STITCH

see page 92

TRAME

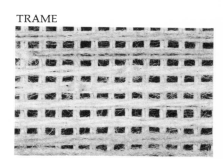

see page 89

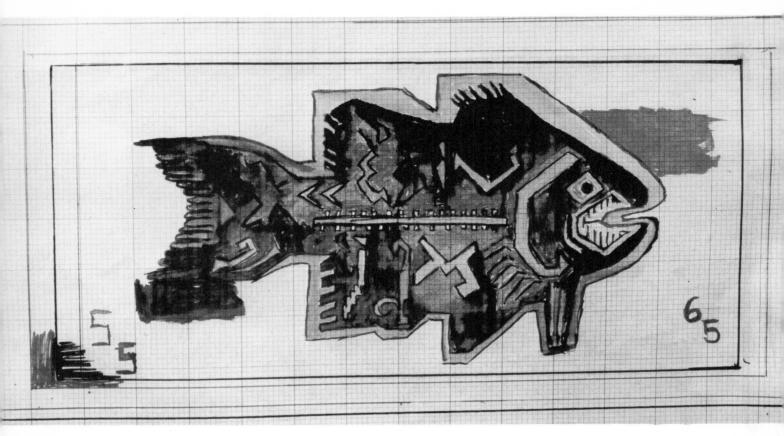

LAZY KNIT

see Reverse Half-Cross, page 89

FRINGE

see page 116

Stitch. It is also very useful in multicolored or toned pieces—you use the same colors that you will use in the regular stitching, so you can get a clear idea of how they will harmonize. Tramé is easy to do and well worth the little extra time it takes. This is also true of fringe, and I added one of silk and wool on each pillow. In addition to making them look larger, it is a nice finishing touch.

If all the animals I have stitched could be counted, I am sure they would fill a small zoo. I did a lion in oranges, yellows, and reds, and a second leopard (see page 40), converting this version into a night scene simply by changing the colors and texture of the background. Another pillow depicted a single frog on a toadstool (page 41). The body was executed in petit point, the background in Lazy Knit (Reverse Half-Cross), and I used Mosaic Stitch to get the bumpy texture of the toadstool. When I worked a second monkey on the branch of a tree (see page 57), I again separated the threads of a penelope canvas and split the silk for the figure. Around it, I alternated rows of blue and white stitching to make a soft transition to the blue background (the swirling pattern of the rows is a background technique I learned in rug hooking).

Since I am speaking of animal designs, may I repeat how helpful children's books are? Many of the stories are about animals. Each has great individuality and marked character traits—the reluctant dragon, the bashful lion, the faithful dog, and so on. The illustrator's object is to capture these qualities in his drawings, and it is amazing to see how successful they have been. Should you want to do designs of this sort in needlepoint and not feel confident about doing your own drawings, you can simply trace onto graph paper any picture that takes your fancy, and work from that. You will probably discover, as I did, that you gradually get bolder and bolder about departing from your sources, until you find you are working entirely on your own.

In the summer of 1965 I was appearing in Shaw's *Candida* in Palo Alto. I became fascinated with the art of the Americas of the pre-Columbian period. The original designs on which I based three pieces I did were so beautiful that I felt it would be near desecration to tamper with them—I could not improvise on compositions so artistically perfect. I simply laid them out on my graph paper and transferred them to canvas exactly as they were (see page 53).

One was a fish, which I found in a photograph of a fragment of ancient Peruvian fabric. I intended, at the beginning, to use a hot red background for the figure. As the work progressed, however, I realized that the red was too strong and might overwhelm the design. It is also not the easiest color to live with. When I had completed the body of the fish in shades of green, yellow, brown, rust, and touches of pale blue silk, I decided that black would make the most effective background and would also blend with almost any decor. I inserted

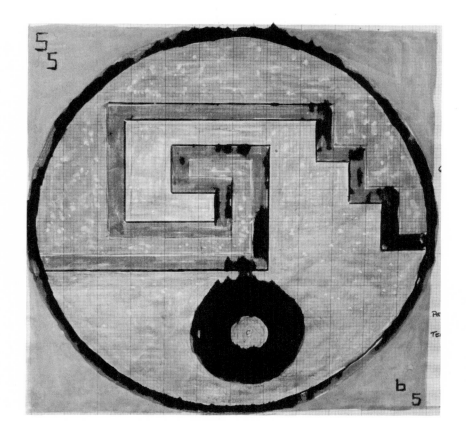

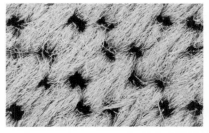

MOSAIC STITCH

see page 90

51

CHECKER STITCH

see page 96

PARISIAN STITCH

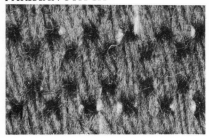

see page 107

the fish, which was petit point done on a mono 32, into a penelope 12-24 canvas and worked the black background in Lazy Knit (Reverse Half-Cross), with a band of bright scarlet in simple Scotch Stitch to set it off.

The second of my pre-Columbian designs—the one that looks a little like a whale (or a mad, old-fashioned iron)—was inspired by a Peruvian clay vessel. I stitched the figure on a mono 28 and inserted it into a mono 16 on which I did the background in Tent Stitch, in pale beige wool. The border is a two-toned Checker Stitch of beige and rust-colored wool mixed with silk.

Finally, I did a very modern-looking abstract design that I found on an Aztec shield. Because one is working on the square meshes of canvas, it is impossible to make a perfect circle in needlepoint. I tried to diminish the squareness by using a pale, muted beige for the corners of the canvas, and this actually enhanced the circular shape of the motif. Since the design was very simple, I used a variety of stitches: Tent, Gobelin, Mosaic, and Parisian. The canvas was a penelope 12-24, and I separated the threads to do the small circles.

In the autumn following my "pre-Columbian period," I was scheduled to start rehearsals for the National Repertory Theater (NRT). We were to make a long cross-country tour, which I was willing to do because it gave me an opportunity to play two parts I probably never would have a chance to do otherwise. One was Mrs. Malaprop, that marvelous garbler of the English language in Sheridan's great comedy of manners, *The Rivals;* the other was Constance, the fey madwoman with an imaginary·dog, in Giradoux's *The Madwoman of Chaillot.*

I knew that I had better provide myself with enough needlepoint projects to fill the time I would spend traveling and waiting to go on stage. One of the pieces started by being especially troublesome, but turned out to be especially rewarding. It was a charming little monkey. I first saw this character just before we went into rehearsal. I was passing the window of one of the antique shops that line New York's Third Avenue, and there was the most enchanting figurine of a mama monkey carrying a baby monkey. I had already done the jungle-monkey pillow, but I wanted to try a portrait head of one. The mama charmed me, and I looked forward to the new challenge she would present. I had worked from pictures and from my imagination. Now I would attempt to capture in stitchery the look and spirit of a three-dimensional subject.

Throughout the weeks of rehearsal I sketched and sketched and sketched. The results were disastrous. I couldn't get the expression. I tried looking at dozens of reference pictures of monkeys: nothing helped. I could not capture my model on paper. That monkey was as enigmatic as the Mona Lisa.

I took the little creature along when we left on the tour and doodled drawings of her as we crossed the country. By the time we arrived in San Francisco I was so exasperated that I was ready to consign her to a watery grave in the Pacific. One rainy afternoon I started to sketch, telling myself it was absolutely the last time I would waste on it. I had

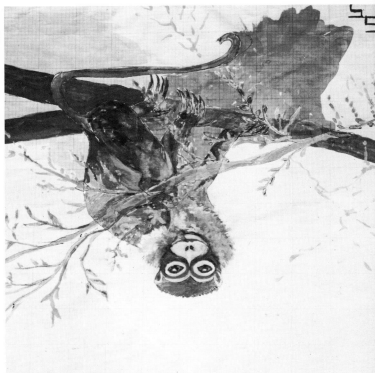

studied the figure so hard for so long that I didn't even bother to look at it. The head then seemed to pop onto the graph paper, and it was right.

The little monster had been so elusive that I decided to celebrate her capture by making her the subject of the most complicated piece I had yet attempted. I would go a step beyond the use of two canvases and try my hand at three. I reasoned that it could not be much more difficult: it was simply an amplification of what I had already accomplished. This fortunately proved to be correct.

As usual, I started with the eyes. I wanted them to be especially expressive, so I did them in silk petit point on a mono 32. I un-

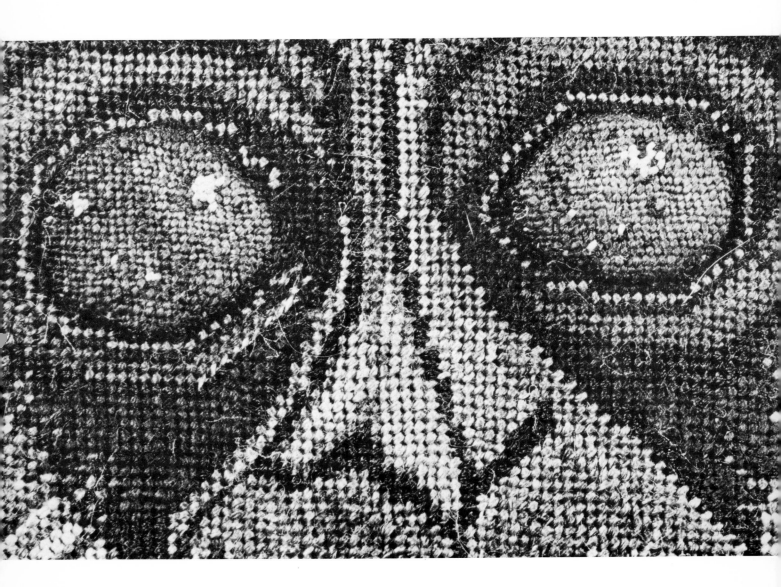

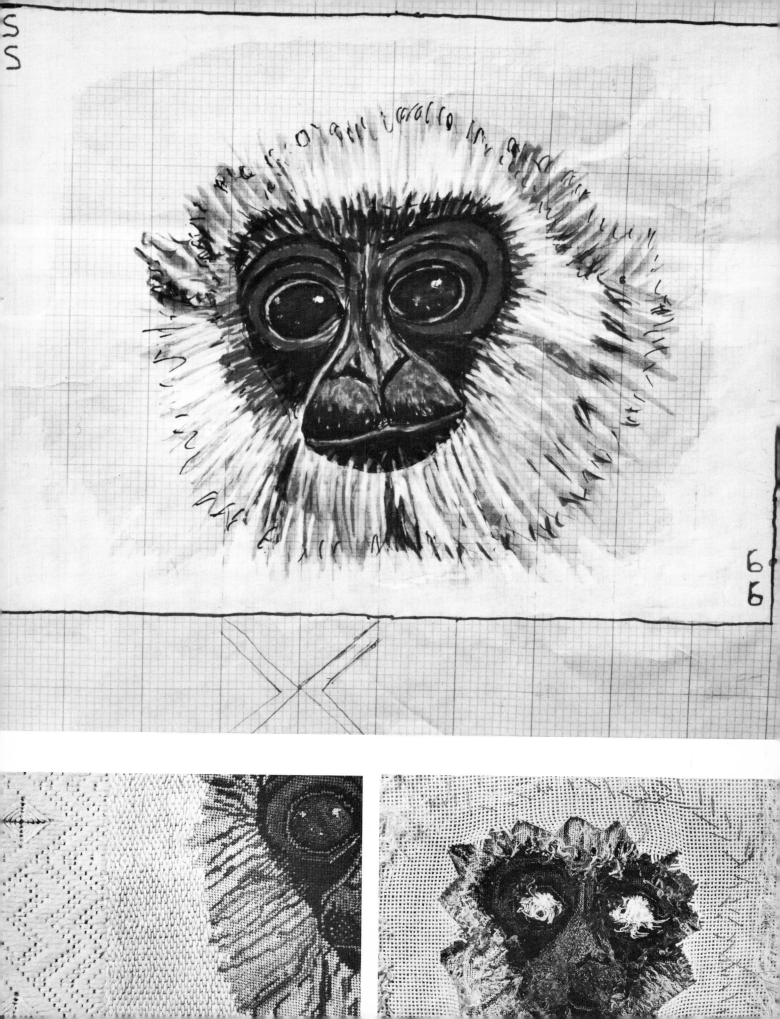

HUNGARIAN STITCH

see page 104

raveled the edges and wove the threads into a mono 18. On this I did the rest of the head and the inner part of the background, also in silk petit point. This canvas in turn I inserted into a mono 14 on which I did the broad border in white silk and wool, using a combination of Bargello and Hungarian Stitch.

While I was working on the piece, my cousin, Dr. Albert Sabin, visited me. He looked at both the sketch and the unfinished canvas. I thought I was in for a lecture on simians—who knew more about monkeys than the man who had used them in perfecting his polio vaccine? To my astonishment, he was very enthusiastic. He said, "That's a perfect Rhesus monkey!"

This cross-country jaunt over, I again hit the road, this time to tour as the mother in *Barefoot in the Park*. We were supposed to play only in the northeastern part of the country, but somehow we managed to get as far west as Colorado Springs and as far southwest as San Antonio. It was what is known in the theater as a bus-and-truck tour. This means that the entire company of actors and technicians travels from engagement to engagement in a bus, while the scenery, props, and costumes follow (or precede) them in a truck. For those who have never made one of these tours, I can only describe it as the closest thing to an authentic gypsy caravan this side of old Bohemia. The only things missing are the fortune tellers and the tambourines. This is not an altogether original observation—the chorus kids, who drift from musical to musical, often spending more time traveling than in any given place, actually refer to themselves as "gypsies." I contributed no small part to the Romany atmosphere of the *Barefoot* tour. A whole row of seats had to be removed from the bus to make room for my clutter of needlepoint and dogs.

The animal world continued to occupy me. I did another giraffe design, this time including two of the graceful animals. They are more or less lolling around, one of them holding an anemone in his mouth. I am sure no giraffe ever looked twice at an anemone. My motivation for bringing them together was the same as for the strawberries—I like anemones.

This pair of giraffes ran away with me. My original intention was to do the animals in petit point on separated threads of penelope 14-28, then insert them into a large-gauge canvas. Unfortunately, I left a lot of space around them, and once I started, I couldn't resist finishing the entire piece in silk on the same canvas. The background is a combination of orange, red, and yellow, with touches of green and beige, done in Half-Cross on toned Tramé. The border is Scotch Stitch in the same orange, red, and yellow (see preceding page).

You might suspect that it was the caravan nature of our tour that inspired me to do next the scrawny camel with the distrusting eye. Actually, the idea was suggested by a pen-and-ink drawing that dated back to the Italian Renaissance. I used only one canvas, a mono 16. I combined many different tints for shading and highlighting, but the sandy color of camel and desert predominates. I split the wool for the body in order to be able to shade more subtly. I also added a lively

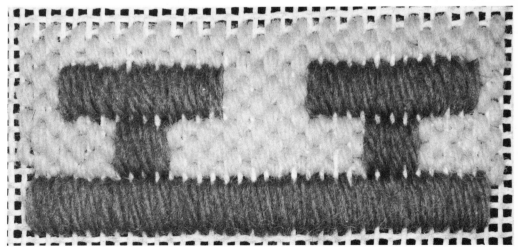

touch of bright red silk in the bridle, repeating the color in a row of Tent Stitch edging just inside the border. The sky is Straight Gobelin; the sand dunes are Bargello, with striations of color; and the border is a combination of Straight Gobelin and Brick Stitch (see page 56).

Shortly after the camel tapestry was completed, the tour came to an end. Returning to New York, I joined the Broadway company of *Barefoot*, replacing Ilka Chase in the same role I had played on the road. Ilka was leaving the show to go off on safari (I felt I had just come back from one!). By coincidence, she is also an ardent needle-worker, and she left behind some unfinished work to be completed by our wonderful wardrobe mistress, Jean Johnson—another enthusiast. Jean often came to visit in my dressing room, and she watched the entire process I went through in making several pieces, from graph-paper sketches to the finished works.

One of these depicted a turtle sniffing a strawberry plant. I was trying for a light and decorative feeling in it. The eye, leaves, and strawberries were done in petit point on separated threads of a penel-ope 14-28, and I sewed a simulated pearl and black beads on the eye and crystal beads on the berries. I then wove these sections into a penelope 10-20 and stitched the rest of the piece. I wanted the shell to have a gay abstract design. I separated the threads of the canvas and split the wool, which made it possible to get all sorts of color combinations by mixing gold, bright red, and bright orange with lots of green, black, and brown. The background is in a mustard-colored Scotch Stitch reversed (Variation #2), with muted gold inner stitches to fill in the spaces and create highlights. The border is Straight Gobelin.

I also worked on a white owl, again using two canvases. The eyes, beak, and claws are petit point on separated threads of a penelope 14-28. I inserted these into a penelope 10-20 and, to make the bird stand out boldly, did the background in two-toned Diagonal Tent Stitch of red and yellow wool. The border, in the same colors, is Slanting Gobelin with accents of Tent Stitch.

Jean Johnson looked on with a great deal of interest. When I asked if she would like to learn how to do a piece from scratch, she eagerly assented. She told me that she came of Swedish stock and had always wanted to do a design based on the Swedish coat of arms. What had held her back was the high cost of having the canvas painted by a professional needlework shop. I was delighted to help: this was my first opportunity to put into words everything I had discovered since my first blundering start with the St. Francis prayer.

We began with a reproduction of the coat of arms, enlarged to the right size for tracing onto graph paper. When I say "we," I mean Jean. I simply stood by and gave her instructions; the labor was entirely hers. But I was almost as pleased as she when she completed a beautiful piece and went on to do a second, this one of the Danish coat of arms. I never had to do a single stitch. Jean knew the rudiments of needle-point, and just by discussing what could be done with variations on what she already knew, I helped her to the point at which she was ready to embark on her own, original designs.

SCOTCH STITCH—VARIATION #2

see page 95

SLANTING GOBELIN STITCH

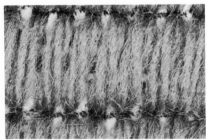

see page 97

For Jean, the desire to branch out started with a coat of arms. It must be obvious from the catalog of pieces in this chapter that working on animals was the stepping-stone for me. Although I first came to do so many of them because they were requested, they proved to be perfectly suited to my particular taste and style. In fact, it was in large part through doing them that my style evolved. Discovering new techniques as I encountered new problems greatly increased the scope of my work; for instance, stumbling onto the method of weaving smaller canvases into larger ones enabled me to combine the most flamboyant stitchery with the most delicate petit point.

The point is that it doesn't matter what one's subject is. Each person who tries needlepoint—whether she traces designs or invents them—will gradually find what is congenial to her and develop an individual style. The fun is the secret that, though it looks so complicated, it is all really very easy to do.

4. And Some People Like Pugs

I cannot tell the whole story of my needlepoint without briefly digressing to the other relatively new passion in my life: pugs! Both began to play increasingly important parts in my life at about the same time—the late 1950s. It was only natural that these delightful little dogs should also become the inspiration for several pieces of needlepoint.

But I must go back to the first time that I met a real live pug. I had seen them in paintings, drawings, old postcards, porcelains, and the like, but it never occurred to me that the breed still existed until Lena Horne and her husband, Lennie Hayton, returned from England with an adorable, bouncing little fawn puppy. The vision of him haunted me for a long time. I had owned many dogs—Dobermans, dachshunds, even a bulldog. But I felt that with my commuting between Hollywood and New York, to say nothing of the tours, I could not assume the kind of responsibility imposed by owning an animal. After seeing the pug, however, I knew that if I were ever again to have a dog, it would have to be a pug.

In 1957 I was in California to do a television play, *The Man From Seventh Avenue*. Every day I lunched together with my co-stars, Patricia Neal and Walter Slezak, and every day, on our way from the rehearsal studios to the restaurant, we passed a pet shop. There Pat and Walter would always lose me for a few minutes while I pored over the litter of pugs in the window. One of them must have bought me the moment she saw me. She seemed to be waiting every time I passed, and she stared with such an appealing look in her eyes that I felt myself losing my heart to her. Finally, I had to give in and buy her.

I named her Madam Oi-Vingh. We had several winter stock engagements together, as well as the entire national tour of *Auntie Mame*. Unfortunately, for all her friskiness, she was not a very strong dog. She died when she was only fourteen months old. I was shattered. I, who until Madam came along had thought myself so self-sufficient, began to experience the most acute loneliness. I wondered if I dared to get another dog and leave myself open to the terrible possibility pug of a second loss. I couldn't do it! I would not buy a pug—I would buy *two* pugs. Then, if anything were to happen to one, I would still have the other.

One had the impressive registered name of Aquilas Goliath. To me he was always just plain Mister Oi-Vingh, and when the female arrived, she was Madam-Too. Mister and Madam went wherever I went and rapidly became a very important part of my life. Once they were introduced, there were no objections to them either from friends or from members of the companies in which I acted. After a few years of trouping around with me, Mister and Madam made their debuts onstage. I was playing in *Kind Sir*, and the director prevailed upon me to let them appear. They were as well behaved onstage as off.

My concern with pugs naturally led to doing them in needlepoint. The first piece I did was a portrait of Mister. All that stood between Mister and competition in dog shows was his floppy ears. With my needle I corrected nature's error and straightened them. This piece was destined for the collection of the Duchess of Windsor, who is also a pug fancier.

Strange as it may seem to put them in one category, I have similar feelings about my needlepoint and my dogs. Collectively, they opened a brand new world to me at a time when I might have started to wonder how I had gotten into the rut that life sometimes seems to become at middle age. One of the wildest and most stimulating periods of my life began when I acquired Captain Midnight, my first black pug. For me it was another case of love at first sight. Cappy was less impetuous, even at six weeks. He looked me over very carefully before making up his mind that I would do. After a half-century of living, it was extraordinary that a little black beast could bring me so much excitement.

To begin with, Cappy was responsible for introducing me to the Duchess of Windsor. She learned, from a mutual friend, that I owned a black pug; at the time, she had only fawns. So Cappy and I were invited to meet her at lunch.

It poured the day we were to go. I called my friend to say that I was reluctant to take Cappy out in that kind of weather. After all, he was only three months old. She replied, "Then don't bother going. It's not you she wants to meet." This certainly ranked my social position in relation to Cappy's. I found a brightly colored plaid stole in which to wrap him, and we went to lunch. It must have been love at first sight for the Duchess, too—for she soon acquired a black pug of her own.

When Cappy was six months old, I decided to enter him in a few dog shows just to see what he could do. He did very well: even at that early age he took several awards. He also joined Mister and Madam in the theater. He made his stage debut in the NRT production of *The*

Rivals—I made my entrance as Mrs. Malaprop with all three pugs in tow. I knew Mister and Madam would be fine: they were already veterans. I was a little apprehensive about the Captain, but I need not have been. He displayed all the aplomb with those audiences that he did in the dog shows.

Cappy finished his championship at quite a young age. He has since won the respect of judges everywhere and become one of the top winning black pug champions in the country. Of course, Cappy also became the subject of a piece of needlepoint. Actually, what I did was combine his features with those of his great mother, Smudgepot. I used this portrait on a cushion commissioned as a birthday present, which gave me the inevitable deadline. Meeting it proved to be quite a challenge.

Cappy was a hard dog to show because despite the beauty of his black coat, it could not be seen unless the light was good. His coloring

caused a similar problem for me when I started to design the needle-point. How was I to get expression and depth into a black head with black markings? And how was I to achieve the highlighting? To use white on inky black would make the face look grotesque. The design was truly a study in black on black.

I took many photographs and did many sketches before I found the solution. Dark blues, grays, and browns would serve well for the highlights. In addition, if I showed Cappy smiling, the teeth and red tongue would provide the bolder definition that was needed. It was a nasty trick to play on Cappy. Smiling is one of the things a show dog is trained never to do in the ring.

I did the head in Tent Stitch on a mono 24 canvas, adding a rust-colored background. This I inserted into a mono 18 on which I worked two borders, also in rust; the inner was Straight Gobelin, the outer Old Florentine. The piece was finished well before the deadly deadline —or so I thought. Then my client spoke a few words that spelled disaster. "Oh no," she said. "It's too small."

Fortunately I was well supplied with rust-colored silk and wool. All I had to do was insert the work in a third canvas, make another border, and finish the pillow off with a fringe. There was one problem, though— I had a contract to do Tennessee Williams' *The Glass Menagerie* in summer stock, about a hundred miles from New York City. Since I had already played the part of Amanda, I only had to brush up on the lines, rather than learn them from the beginning. I could rehearse during the day and spend the evenings working on the needlepoint. When I finished it, I naively thought, I would simply drive to the city in a leisurely way, hand over the piece, and drive back in time for a nap before the evening performance. It would even be a pleasant break in my routine.

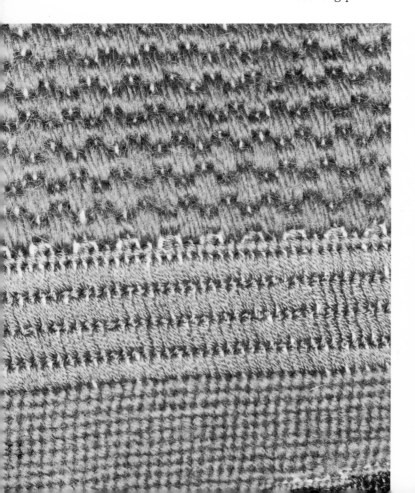 

Although my son helped, packing the car to leave for New Jersey was somewhat complicated. I was traveling with all three dogs. In one hand I carried a plastic bag containing the designs and materials for several other pieces I was planning; in the other I clutched a bag filled with the silk and wool needed to complete the new border. Finally, everything was stowed away. I kissed Jody goodbye and began the journey.

That same night I unpacked and began to weave the finished part of the work into the larger-gauge canvas, a mono 14. It took me a little longer than I had anticipated because it was difficult to line up the threads of the two canvases. I managed to finish making the insert, but with the pressures of rehearsal, it was two days before I was able to return to the needlepoint. Opening night was approaching, and so was the deadline. I mapped out a Bargello border on the canvas in indelible ink and carefully counted out the threads. I was ready to begin stitching—except for one small detail.

I couldn't find the bag with the yarn! I turned my room upside down and inside out. It was no use; the bag simply was not there. I couldn't call my son to get it to me (assuming I had indeed left it behind by mistake); he had already left on a holiday trip.

Since my arrival there had been steady, torrential rain. It was insanity to consider driving to and from New York in it, especially after a tiring day of rehearsals. Not only did I consider it—I set out to do it. I bundled the three dogs and myself into the car and headed for the city.

I arrived back at the apartment. There, sitting on the table right in the entrance, was the bag I so clearly remembered clutching in my hand. In the tumult of loading and leaving, I had put it on the trunk instead of in it. When I drove away, it fell off. It was just luck that Jody had happened to see it.

I worked furiously through rehearsals and dress rehearsals, trying to make up for lost time. I couldn't do much during the play—I was on-stage almost constantly. We opened on a Tuesday; by Thursday the pillow was supposed to be in the hands of my client. On Wednesday night, after playing two performances, I loaded the still unfinished work, the dogs, and myself back into the car for another trip to New York. It was still pouring. This was the last straw—even Madam lost her composure and howled like a banshee.

When we got home, the pugs rolled up and went to sleep. I was not so fortunate. I had part of the border and the fringe to complete. I plowed on, stopping only to walk the dogs when morning came and with it, finally, the sun. By noon I only had to put on the finishing touches and clip the messy ends from the back. I delivered the canvas at two and drove straight back to New Jersey, arriving at five. I napped until seven and arrived at the theater in time for the evening performance. So much for that pleasant break in routine I had anticipated!

The next major dog subject I did was a gift for a good friend, Mary Pickhardt. The Pickhardts raise championship pugs, and they came to my rescue at a sad time. Mister had died suddenly. The Captain and Madam kept looking at me with eyes filled with recrimination:

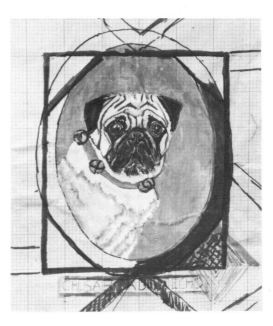

74

all they knew was that I had wrapped him in a blanket and taken him away, and he had never returned. Mary generously offered me Small Wonder, the daughter of one of her great dogs. Wonder turned out to be such a wonderful tonic for all of us that I decided to do a portrait of Echo, her illustrious sire.

Echo's expression was difficult to capture. It may seem to the uninitiated that a pug is a pug is a pug, but as I have said, every animal is an individual. I think I finally got the "look" of Echo.

I used three canvases in executing the piece. The head to the collar is on a mono 32; the body to the inner frame is on a mono 18, and the large outer frame is on a penelope 9-18. The background behind Echo I did in Brick Stitch with mauve silk. The corners of the inner frame are pale orchid and deep purple Cross Stitch (Reverse Half-Cross over Half-Cross) over light blue Tramé, while the inner frame itself is deep purple silk. The outer frame is also Bargello, executed in purple, pink, and blue wools—Mary's favorite colors.

Finishing the canvas was only the beginning. I decided to set it in a tray that would stand on a collapsible luggage rack like one I owned. After I made the bands for it in Herringbone Stitch, using up all the leftover pinks, blues, and purples, I still had to find a tray. I finally located one; all that remained was to get the rack. There was none to be found in all of New York—the only recourse was to use my own. It had to be redone to match the finish of the tray. I removed the paint

HERRINGBONE STITCH

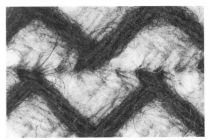

see page 110

and stained the wood dark brown. Over this I put a coat of black-brown and, last, a reddish glaze. Then I steel-wooled, waxed, and buffed the rack and attached the tapes.

It never ceases to amaze me how what starts with needle and canvas often ends up incorporating so many other materials and skills. But the constant challenge is part of what makes needlework an endless source of pleasure.

The other part, of course, is being able to give pleasure to other people. Recently I wanted to express my appreciation of the long friendship I have shared with Jan Miner and Dick Merrell. They also have become "pug people"—they own Little Mistuh, one of the sons of Madam and Mister. I decided to do a miniature to fit in a small Victorian frame.

Little Mistuh was done in petit point on a mono 32 canvas. I used soft beiges accented with blacks and blues for the figure, and worked the background in greens and blues in Diagonal Tent Stitch.

Dick and Jan love the piece—and for me that is the measure of its success. As I look back over the needlework I have done, I realize that I have always felt the same way about it: the only real measure I have of success in any of my work is the pleasure it has given to those who own it.

In a sense, I began doing needlework with a prayer. It seems only right to bring my book full circle with the story of another prayer that I did a very short time ago. It was the endearing prayer of St. Mathilde:

> O God, give unto me by grace
> That obedience which thou hast
> Given to my little dog by nature.

I made the design a very simple one, because I felt the thought did not need any embellishment beyond delicate workmanship. I laid it out on graph paper as usual, then traced it onto a penelope 14-28 canvas.

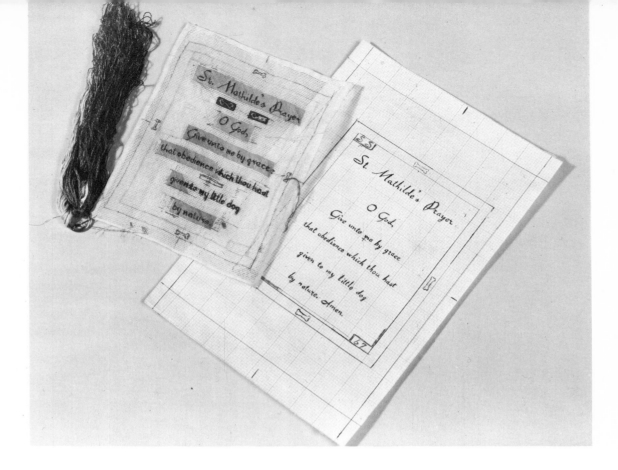

I didn't stop to count the threads. By this time, one would have thought, I would know better. Paper and canvas cannot count. I had not gone far before it was clear that I would have to make adjustments. A comparison of the original design on graph paper and the finished work gives some indication of what I did. I was determined not to start all over again.

I eliminated the "Amen" with which I had planned to end the prayer. Most of the letters, which were petit point done on separated threads, had to be completely realigned. Instead of using dog bones for the frame, I inserted them between the lines to compensate for bad spacing.

The background was done in Scotch Stitch reversed (Variation #2), with the inserted stitches in gold metallic thread; the border in a combination of Herringbone and Gobelin. Finally, I matted the finished piece with the same garnet velvet as the St. Francis prayer.

Through the years, the most important rule I've learned is that, aside from the actual stitchery, there are *no* rules in the design and execution of a piece. In laying one out, if something seems right to you, with a little thought, you can find the way to make it *work* right.

My experiences with needlepoint have given me a sense of accomplishment that has been as rewarding as any success I have ever achieved. The happiness the pieces have given to the people who own them has made me feel very rich indeed. This is what has inspired me to continue, stitch after stitch, with every piece I have ever done. It is also what inspired this book.

St. Mathilde's Prayer

O God,

Give unto me by grace

that obedience which thou hast

given to my little dog

by nature.

5. Basically Two Stitches

The time has come for me to get down to explaining the actual mechanics of the stitches. In wondering about the best way to do this, I naturally thought of my grandmother whose lessons in knitting started me on the road to "needlepointing." She was also a first-rate cook, and spent a lifetime giving out the most complicated recipes. She always started in exactly the same way. She would wipe her hands on her apron, then put the forefinger of her right hand to the pinky of her left hand. A faraway look would come into her eyes, and her audience would wait breathlessly, anticipating the most exotic instructions. Then she would begin to speak very slowly, and she always said the same thing: "First you wash your hands."

My grandmother always made things simple because she got right down to the basics. After all these years of doing needlepoint, I have realized that there are basics here, too. In breaking down the various pieces I have made into their component parts, I discovered that *all* needlepoint is basically two stitches done on two types of canvas. How they are used and put together is what makes it challenging and fun—and gives one the most tremendous sense of accomplishment.

The two basic stitches are a little slanting one and a straight up-and-down one, and these are developed into Mosaic, Scotch, Brick, Old Florentine, Hungarian, Parisian, Bargello, and more—the variations are endless!

The slanting stitch is the more common of the two—it can be used for practically everything. There are three methods of doing it: as Half-Cross, Tent (or Continental) Stitch, and Diagonal Tent Stitch. Although from the front all three look very similar, a glance at the back of the canvas shows the striking differences among them. The Half-Cross gives a very thin backing. It is economical of materials, but it cannot be done on mono-canvas. The Tent Stitch gives more backing. The result is a firmer piece of work and a more pleasant texture on the front. The Diagonal Tent Stitch is the most extravagant. It gives marvelous padding at the back and, I think, a richer texture on the front.

The other basic stitch—the straight up-and-down one—is Gobelin, which is really the old-fashioned Satin Stitch. Gobelin serves a variety of purposes that, at least for me, make it far from secondary. Three notes before I get to the stitches:

Except in a few cases, there is no rule about starting left or right. As for the exceptions, I will caution you as they occur. There are some procedures I follow simply out of habit.

Some people, in giving instructions, count the number of threads over which a stitch is done. I go by meshes. As you can easily see in the illustrations, when *inserting* the needle I count meshes from the mesh where the yarn comes through to the front of the canvas, and when *bringing out* the needle, I count from the mesh where the needle has been inserted.

Finally, except where I have noted otherwise, the stitches can be done on either mono-canvas or penelope.

Back Tuck-In

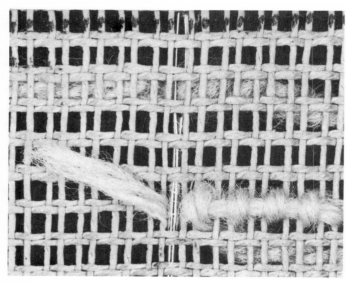

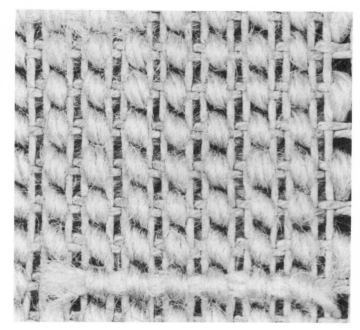

Always start with a neat tuck-in at the back of the canvas. Leave at least an inch of yarn at the back. Hold it there with one hand and make sure the needle covers it as you draw through to the front for five or six stitches. Once work is under way, you can simply weave ends into the back of the stitches or row before. This holds for ending a strand, too, as you can see in the illustrations of the back of the next three stitches.

Back of the Half-Cross Stitch.

Half-Cross Stitch

Front of the Half-Cross Stitch. *This stitch cannot be done on mono-canvas.*

1—Starting at the right, bring needle through to front of canvas. (Don't forget to hold the end of the strand in back for the tuck-in.) Insert needle 1 mesh above and 1 mesh to left; bring it out vertically, 1 mesh directly below. Don't pull the strand too tight—keep it relaxed and puffy. You have accomplished the first stitch!

2—Now, once again, insert needle 1 mesh above and 1 mesh to left; bring it out 1 mesh directly below. Continue to end of row.

4—Row 3: Turn the canvas around again and continue. (Illustration shows position of needle after turning work.)

3—Row 2: Simply turn the work around and continue as above. (Illustration shows position of needle before turning work.)

Tent Stitch

Front of the Tent Stitch.

Back of the Tent Stitch.

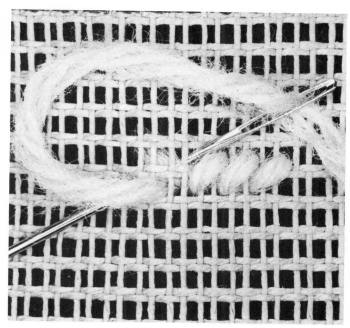

2—Again insert needle 1 mesh above and 1 mesh to right; bring it out 1 mesh below and 2 meshes to left. Continue to end of row.

1—Starting at the right, bring needle through to front of canvas. Insert it 1 mesh above and 1 mesh to right; bring it out 1 mesh below and 2 meshes to left.

3—Insert needle 1 mesh above and 1 mesh to right; bring it out 1 mesh directly below. You are now ready to start Row 2.

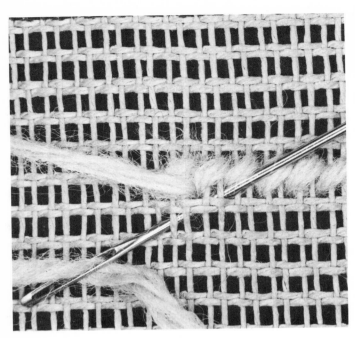

4—Row 2: Turn the work around and continue as in step 2. (Illustration shows position of needle before turning work.)

Back of the Diagonal Tent Stitch.

Diagonal Tent Stitch

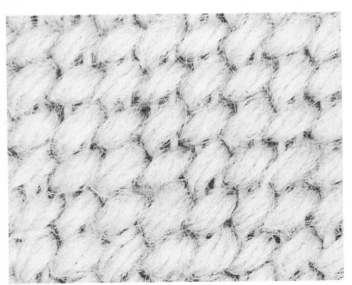

Front of the Diagonal Tent Stitch. This looks a little frightening, but once you get the rhythm, it works quickly. One advantage of the stitch is that it holds its shape well. *You must start this stitch at the upper right corner.*

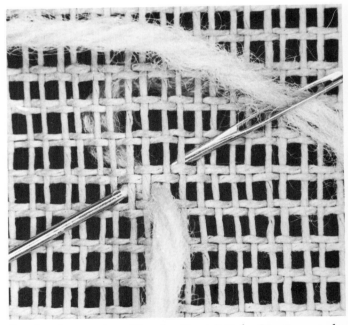

1—This begins just like the Tent Stitch. Starting at the right, bring needle through to front of canvas. Insert it 1 mesh above and 1 mesh to right; bring it out 1 mesh below and 2 meshes to left. Now, go carefully.

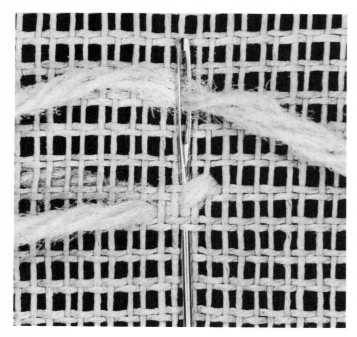

2—Insert needle 1 mesh above and 1 mesh to right; bring it out vertically, 2 meshes directly below.

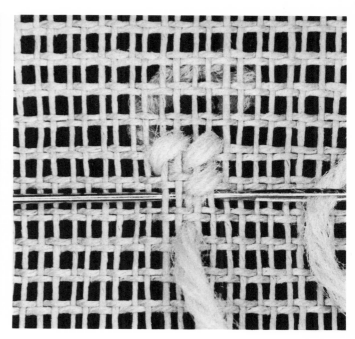

4—Insert needle 1 mesh above and 1 mesh to right; bring it out horizontally, 2 meshes directly to left.

3—Insert needle 1 mesh above and 1 mesh to right; bring it out 2 meshes below and 1 mesh to left.

5—Insert needle 1 mesh above and 1 mesh to right; bring it out horizontally, 2 meshes directly to left.

6—Insert needle 1 mesh above and 1 mesh to right; bring it out 1 mesh below and 2 meshes to left.

When you are working down, the needle is vertical, except for the last stitch, when it is slanted (as in step *3*).

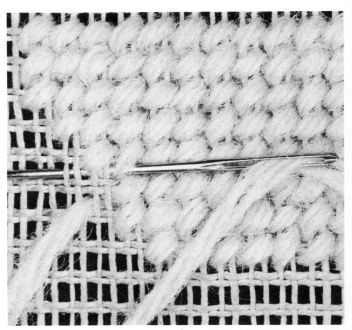

7—Insert needle 1 mesh above and 1 mesh to right; bring it out vertically, 2 meshes directly below.

When you are working up, the needle is horizontal, except for the last stitch, when it is slanted (as in step *6*).

Tramé

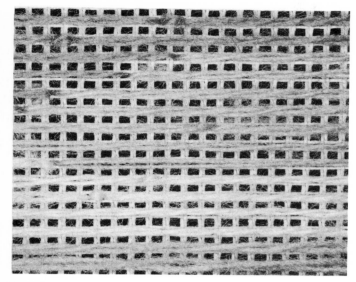

Tramé works best on penelope canvas. It is especially useful as a backing for Half-Cross and for multicolored pieces. Use the same yarns that will be used over the Tramé (unless you want another color to show through). If you are working in wool, split the yarn and use one strand; in silk, use as many strands as are required.

Working from side to side, take long stitches and anchor them with a little backstitch over one mesh. Vary the length of the stitches so that the backstitch doesn't fall in the same place in every row—if this happens, a ridge will appear.

Reverse Half-Cross Stitch

The Reverse Half-Cross Stitch is simply the Half-Cross slanted in the other direction. By alternating rows of Half-Cross and Reverse Half-Cross, you get the Lazy Knit Stitch shown here. If you overstitch the Half-Cross with the Reverse Half-Cross, you get the Cross Stitch. Since these stitches are variations of the Half-Cross, *they cannot be done on mono-canvas.*

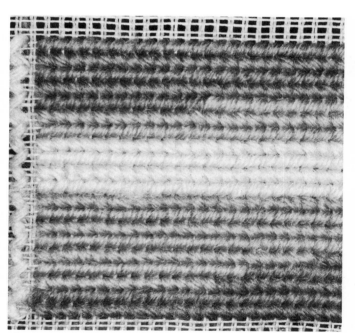

The Lazy Knit Stitch, toned. To prevent mistakes, always make a guide at the edges of the canvas, as shown. Then you can see in which direction the stitches should go, no matter where you begin.

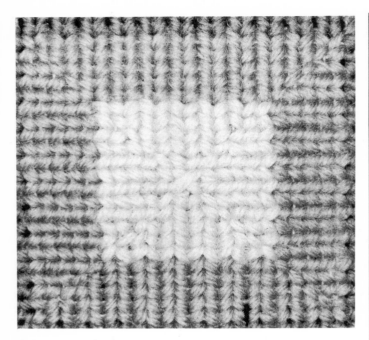

Variation of the Lazy Knit Stitch.

Horizontal Mosaic Stitch

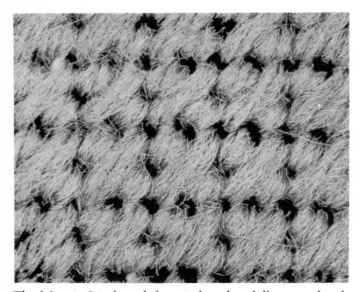

The Mosaic Stitch and the stitches that follow are developments of the Tent Stitch. It is easy to do if you mark off the working area as illustrated in the following pictures.

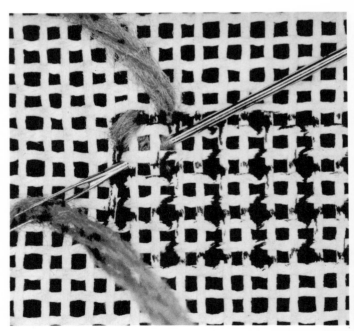

1—Starting at the left, bring needle through to front of canvas. Insert it 1 mesh below and 1 mesh to left; bring it out 1 mesh above and 2 meshes to right.

2—Insert needle 2 meshes below and 2 meshes to left; bring it out 1 mesh above and 2 meshes to right.

3—Insert needle 1 mesh below and 1 mesh to left; bring it out 2 meshes above and 2 meshes to right.

Diagonal Mosaic Stitch

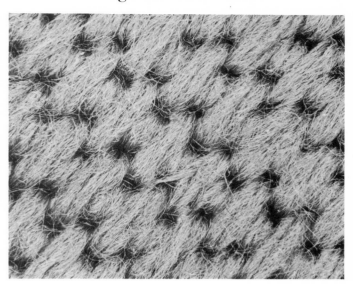

The Diagonal Mosaic Stitch has an easier rhythm than the Horizontal Mosaic. It is lovely done in two or three different shades. Mark off the working area as illustrated in the following pictures.

4—To continue, repeat from step *1*.

1—Starting at the left, bring needle through to front of canvas. Insert it 1 mesh above and 1 mesh to right; bring it out 2 meshes below and 1 mesh to left.

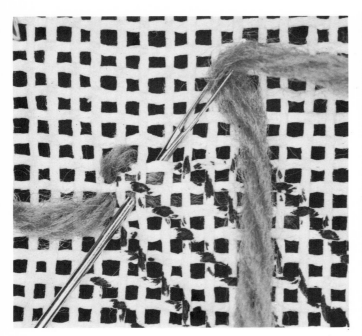

2—Insert needle 2 meshes above and 2 meshes to right; bring it out 2 meshes below and 1 mesh to left.

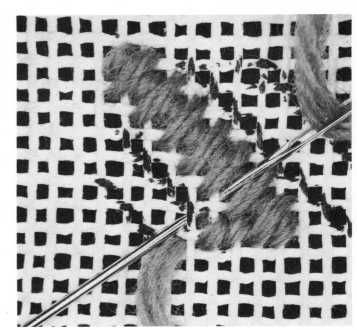

4—Insert needle as in step *3*; bring it out 1 mesh below and 3 meshes to left. To fill in space left between rows, insert needle 1 mesh above and 1 mesh to right; bring it out 1 mesh below and 2 meshes to left (a Tent Stitch). Row 2: insert needle 1 mesh above and 1 mesh to right; bring it out 1 mesh below and 2 meshes to left. Insert needle 2 meshes above and 2 meshes to right; bring it out 1 mesh below and 2 meshes to left. To continue, repeat these two stitches.

Scotch Stitch

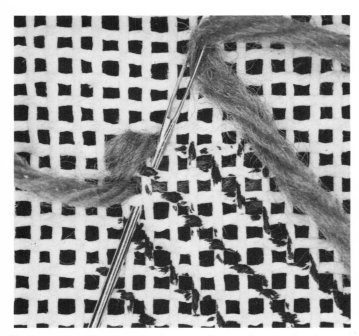

3—Insert needle 1 mesh above and 1 mesh to right; bring it out 2 meshes below and 1 mesh to left. To continue, repeat from step *2*. To begin next row, proceed from step *2* as follows.

The basic Scotch Stitch can be done in squares of 3, 4, 5, or 6 meshes. If the squares are marked off as illustrated in the following pictures, no counting will be necessary once you begin. Scotch Stitch can be done diagonally or horizontally: the basic square is the same for both.

1—Starting at the left, bring needle through to front of canvas. Insert it 1 mesh above and 1 mesh to right; bring it out 2 meshes below and 1 mesh to left.

3—Insert needle 3 meshes above and 3 meshes to right; bring it out 4 meshes below and 3 meshes to left.

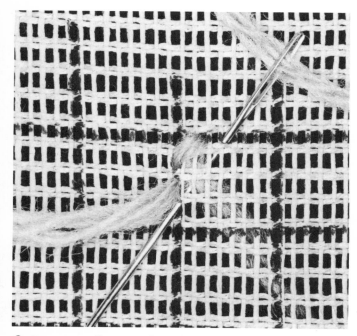

2—Insert needle 2 meshes above and 2 meshes to right; bring it out 3 meshes below and 2 meshes to left.

4—Insert needle 4 meshes above and 4 meshes to right; bring it out 4 meshes below and 3 meshes to left. For the next two stitches, insert needle 3 meshes above and 3 meshes to right; bring it out 3 meshes below and 2 meshes to left; then insert needle 2 meshes above and 2 meshes to right; bring it out 2 meshes below and 1 mesh to left.

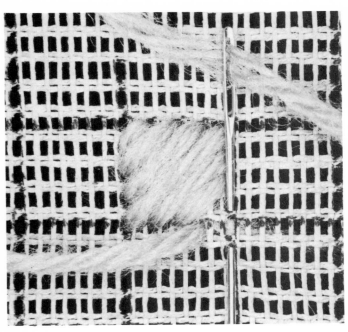

5—To work *diagonally,* complete the basic square by inserting needle 1 mesh above and 1 mesh to right (a Tent Stitch); bring it out 2 meshes directly below.

7—To work *horizontally,* complete the basic square by inserting needle 1 mesh above and 1 mesh to right (as in step 5); bring it out 2 meshes directly above. Then insert needle 1 mesh above and 1 mesh to right; bring it out 2 meshes below and 1 mesh to left. Continue from step 2 to complete square.

6—Insert needle 1 mesh above and 1 mesh to right; bring it out 2 meshes below and 1 mesh to left. Continue from step 2 to complete square.

Scotch Stitch—Variation #1

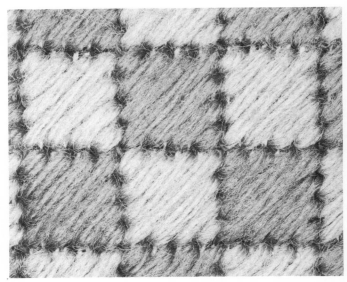

This is simply the Scotch Stitch done diagonally in two colors.

Scotch Stitch—Variation #2

This is Scotch Stitch reversed. The stitch is done diagonally in opposite directions, with stitches added at the corners of the squares. The possible combinations of color are infinite.

Scotch Stitch—Variation #4

Work the stitch diagonally in opposite directions. In each square, use one shade of yarn for steps 1-4 and another shade to complete the square. This has a wonderful parquet effect.

Scotch Stitch—Variation #3

To do this, work the stitch diagonally in opposite directions. Skip step 4 in each square; then fill it in with a contrasting color or shade.

Scotch Stitch—Variation #5

Work the stitch diagonally in opposite directions. In the first square, use one shade of yarn for steps 1-4 and another shade to complete the square; reverse the shades in the second square, and continue alternating.

Scotch Stitch—Variation #6

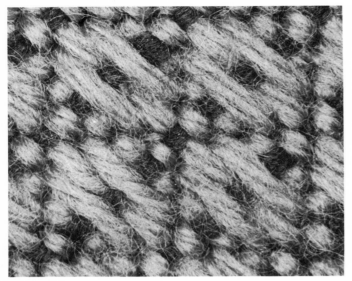

Work the stitch diagonally. Then take yarn in a sharply contrasting color and weave it in and out through the squares.

Checker Stitch

This is usually listed as a separate stitch, but it is simply a combination of Scotch Stitch and either Half-Cross or Tent Stitch. It can be worked horizontally or diagonally, in one color or in any combination of colors. It is very useful for borders and backgrounds because it works up quickly and the texture is very effective.

Scotch Stitch—Variation #7

Work the stitch diagonally in opposite directions. Then outline each square with a simple backstitch.

Straight Gobelin Stitch

The basic, and simplest, of the straight up-and-down stitches is Gobelin. It covers large (or small) areas very quickly, and the texture of it is quite beautiful. Depending on the effect desired, it can be worked over 2, 3, 4, or 5 meshes. It is very easy to do if you mark the canvas as illustrated in the following pictures.

1—Starting at the left, bring needle through to front of canvas a desired number of meshes below the edge (in the illustration, 5 meshes). Insert needle 5 meshes directly above; bring it out 5 meshes below and 1 mesh to right.

2—Insert needle 5 meshes directly above; bring it out 5 meshes below and 1 mesh to right. Continue to end of row.

Slanting Gobelin Stitch

Slanting Gobelin may sound like just another variation of the basic slanting stitch, but as you can see, it looks very different from the Half-Cross and Tent Stitches. Mark off the working area as illustrated in the following pictures.

1—Starting at the left, bring needle through to front of canvas a desired number of meshes below the edge (in the illustration, 4 meshes). Insert needle 4 meshes above and 1 mesh to right; bring it out 4 meshes directly below.

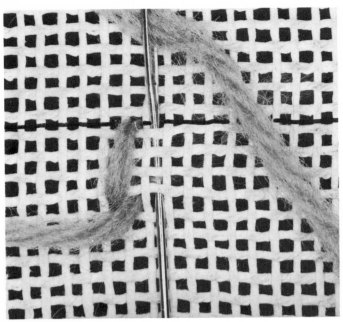

2—Insert needle 4 meshes above and 1 mesh to right; bring it out 4 meshes directly below. Continue to end of row.

Back of Brick Stitch # 1.

Brick Stitch #1

Front of Brick Stitch #1. Like Gobelin, the Brick Stitch is very useful for filling in areas such as backgrounds. Brick Stitch #1 works best on mono-canvas.

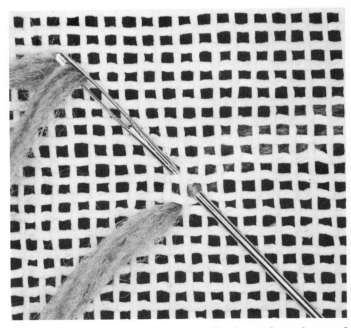

1—Starting at the left, bring needle through to front of canvas 4 meshes below the edge. Insert needle 2 meshes directly above; bring it out 1 mesh below and 1 mesh to right.

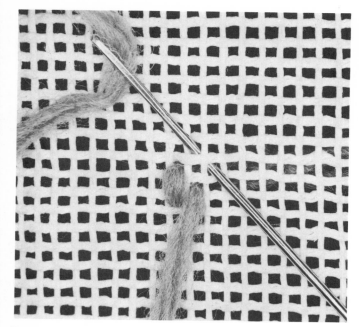

2—Insert needle 2 meshes directly above; bring it out 1 mesh below and 1 mesh to right.

4—Insert needle 2 meshes directly above; bring it out 1 mesh below and 1 mesh to right. To continue, repeat from step *3*. To begin next row, proceed from step *4* as follows.

3—Insert needle 2 meshes directly below; bring it out 1 mesh above and 1 mesh to right.

5—Insert needle 2 meshes directly below; bring it out 2 meshes directly below. Row 2: insert needle 2 meshes directly above; bring it out 1 mesh below and 1 mesh to left.

6—Insert needle 2 meshes directly above; bring it out 1 mesh below and 1 mesh to left. To continue, turn the work around and repeat from step 3. (Illustration shows position of needle before turning work.)

Back of Brick Stitch #2.

Brick Stitch #2

Front of Brick Stitch #2. This has the same effect as Brick Stitch #1, but I prefer it because it gives more backing.

1—Starting at the left, bring needle through to front of canvas 2 meshes below the edge. Insert needle 2 meshes directly above; bring it out 2 meshes below and 2 meshes to right. Continue to end of row.

2—Insert needle 2 meshes directly above; bring it out 3 meshes below and 1 mesh to left.

Old Florentine Stitch

If you mark off the canvas as illustrated in the following pictures, you will not need to count after the first few stitches.

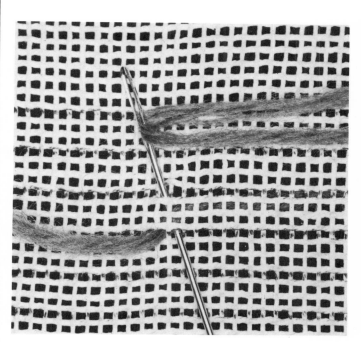

3—Row 2: insert needle 2 meshes directly above; bring it out 2 meshes below and 2 meshes to left. Continue to end of row.

1—Starting at the left, bring needle through to front of canvas 7 meshes below the edge. Insert needle 3 meshes directly above; bring it out 3 meshes below and 1 mesh to right.

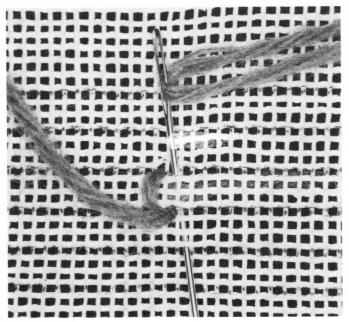

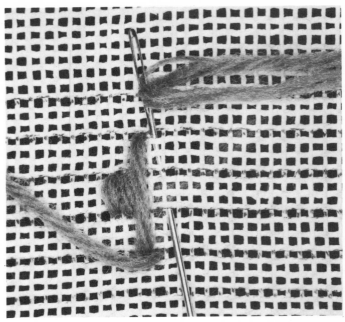

2—Insert needle 3 meshes directly above; bring it out 6 meshes below and 1 mesh to right.

4—Insert needle 9 meshes directly above; bring it out 6 meshes below and 1 mesh to right.

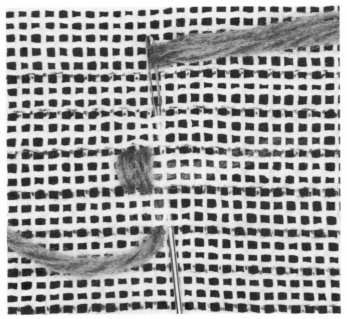

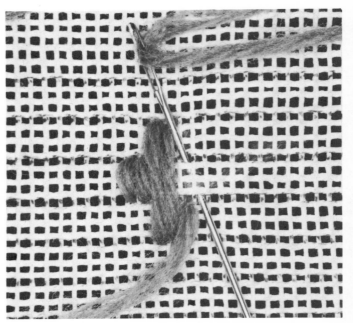

3—Insert needle 9 meshes directly above; bring it out 9 meshes below and 1 mesh to right.

5—Insert needle 3 meshes directly above; bring it out 3 meshes below and 1 mesh to right. To continue, repeat from step 2. To begin next row, proceed as follows.

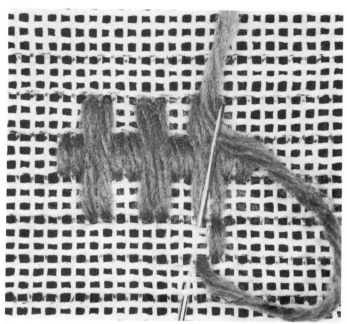

6—Insert needle 3 meshes directly above; bring it out 9 meshes below and 2 meshes to left.

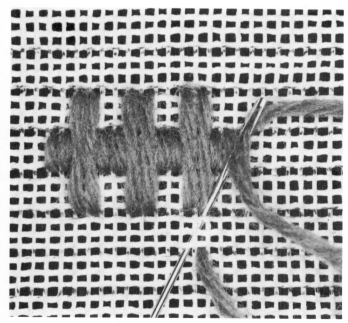

7—Row 2: insert needle 3 meshes directly above; bring it out 3 meshes below and 1 mesh to left.

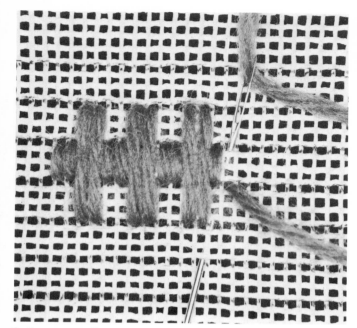

8—Insert needle 3 meshes directly above; bring it out 6 meshes below and 1 mesh to left. To continue, repeat from step 2, only working to the left.

Old Florentine—Variation

The Old Florentine Stitch done in two colors.

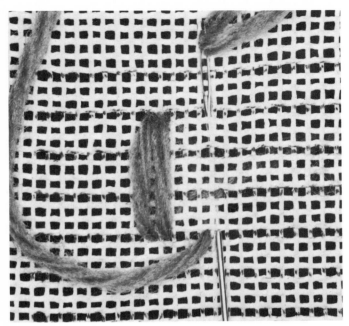

1—Color 1: bring needle through to front of canvas 10 meshes below the edge. Insert needle 10 meshes directly above; bring it out 10 meshes below and 1 mesh to right. Continue to end of row.

Hungarian Stitch

The Hungarian Stitch is very good for backgrounds and as a fill-in for Bargello. This stitch works best on mono-canvas.

2—Color 2: bring needle through to front of canvas 7 meshes below the edge and 2 meshes to left of first stitch in color 1. Insert needle 3 meshes directly above; bring it out 3 meshes below and 3 meshes to right. Continue to end of row.

1—Starting at left, bring needle through to front of canvas 3 meshes below the edge. Insert needle 2 meshes directly above; bring it out 3 meshes below and 1 mesh to right.

2—Insert needle 4 meshes directly above; bring it out 3 meshes below and 1 mesh to right.

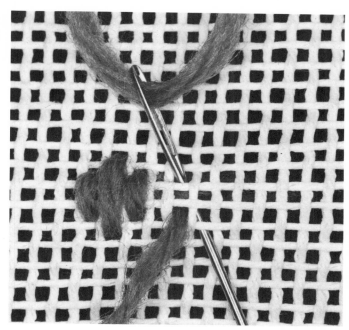

4—Insert needle 2 meshes directly above; bring it out 3 meshes below and 1 mesh to right. To continue, repeat from step 2. To begin next row, proceed from step 2 as follows.

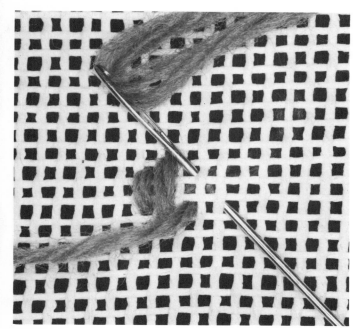

3—Insert needle 2 meshes directly above; bring it out 2 meshes below and 2 meshes to right.

5—Insert needle 2 meshes directly above; bring it out 4 meshes directly below.

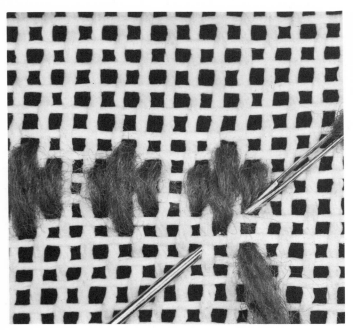

6—Row 2: insert needle 2 meshes directly above; bring it out 2 meshes below and 2 meshes to left.

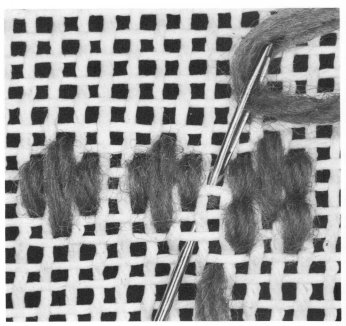

8—Insert needle 4 meshes directly above; bring it out 3 meshes below and 1 mesh to left.

7—Insert needle 2 meshes directly above; bring it out 3 meshes below and 1 mesh to left.

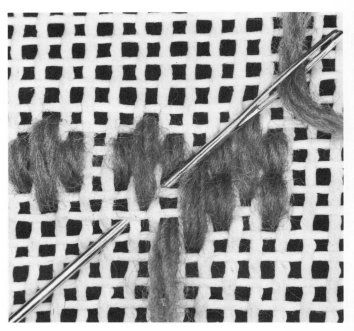

9—Insert needle 2 meshes directly above; bring it out 2 meshes below and 2 meshes to left. To continue, repeat from step *6*.

Hungarian Stitch—Variation

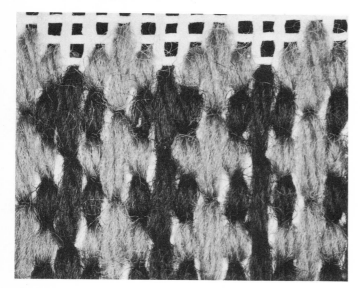

The Hungarian Stitch done in two colors.

Parisian Stitch

The Parisian Stitch is similar to the Hungarian Stitch, but the effect is more close knit. It is also good for backgrounds and as a fill-in for Bargello. The first two steps are exactly like the beginning of the Hungarian Stitch.

1—Starting at left, bring needle through to front of canvas 3 meshes below the edge. Insert needle 2 meshes directly above; bring it out 3 meshes below and 1 mesh to right.

2—Insert needle 4 meshes directly above; bring it out 3 meshes below and 1 mesh to right.

3—Insert needle 2 meshes directly above; bring it out 3 meshes below and 1 mesh to right.

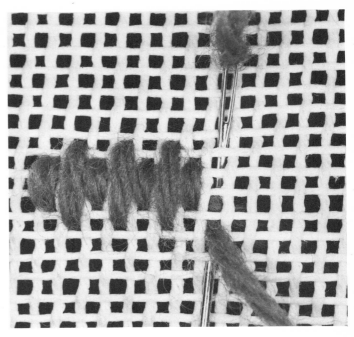

5—Insert needle 4 meshes directly above; bring it out 6 meshes directly below.

4—To continue, repeat from step 2. To begin next row, proceed from step 2 as follows.

6—Row 2: insert needle 2 meshes directly above; bring it out 3 meshes below and 1 mesh to left. To continue, repeat from step 2, only working to the left.

Parisian Stitch—Variation

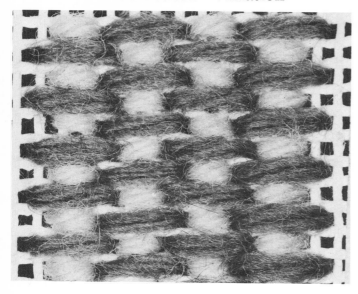

The Parisian Stitch done in two colors.

Bargello Stitch

Bargello (also called Florentine or Flame Stitch) is actually just an extension of the Hungarian and Parisian Stitches. The potential for variation is fascinating—I don't believe there can ever be two pieces of Bargello that are exactly alike. For me, needlepoint becomes most exciting with Bargello—it is the place to let your eye and imagination have free rein.

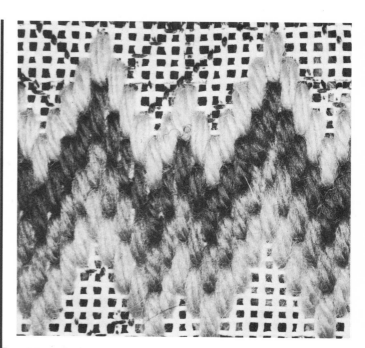

Although it looks so complicated, Bargello is all the simplest up-and-down stitchery. There are absolutely no rules for it—the sequence of stitches depends on the pattern and effect you want, and it is difficult to draw or make a hard-and-fast design for it. I can only suggest the procedure that has been of great help to me.

Draw some guidelines with a pencil and ruler, being careful to make the diagonals hit the intersections of the threads of the canvas (that is, the corners of the meshes). Mark off as many steps as seem necessary; it will save your constantly having to count spaces as you work. Usually, when one row or pattern is completed, all the rest will fall into place quite automatically.

If you reverse the Bargello zig-zag, the points will always meet, and the most interesting diamond shapes will emerge. With these you can improvise all manner of stitchery and coloring.

Squares, triangles, and diamonds will come out evenly if you use the center of the piece as a focal point and count out from it to the right, left, top, bottom, and so on. Then, with the ruler, draw diagonal lines criss-crossing these shapes. Smaller figures will emerge in larger ones, and you can repeat the process exactly or vary the lines to create all sorts of intriguing patterns.

Herringbone #1

Herringbone and Fringe are two stitches that don't fall into any category. I am not sure they can properly be called needlepoint, so I call them "odds." Although they may seem complicated, once mastered they work very quickly and are lovely.

The illusion of depth created by shading or coloring in Herringbone is very pleasing. The stitch can be done in as many as six different colors. For purposes of illustration in black and white here, four shades of gray, from very light to charcoal, are used.

Herringbone works best on penelope. Marking the canvas is a great help: draw horizontal lines every 4 meshes, a vertical line 4 meshes to the right of the starting point, and vertical lines every 6 meshes after that, as in the following pictures.

If you are doing a border or other small area, the ordinary method of tucking in will work perfectly well. However, if the area to be covered is large, don't tuck in at the beginning and end of each row, which makes the edges very bulky. Instead, weave the ends in and out for 5 or 6 meshes. *Herringbone must be worked from left to right.*

ROW 1, COLOR 1
1—Starting at the left, bring needle through to front of canvas 4 meshes below top edge. Insert needle 1 mesh below and 1 mesh to right; bring it out 1 mesh directly to left.

3—Insert needle 4 meshes below and 4 meshes to right; bring it out 1 mesh directly to left. To continue, repeat from step 2. To begin next row, proceed from step 3 as follows.

2—Insert needle 4 meshes above and 4 meshes to right; bring it out 1 mesh directly to left.

ROW 2, COLOR 1 (OR 2)
1—Bring needle through to front 3 meshes below top edge (1 mesh above first stitch in Row 1). Insert needle 2 meshes below and 2 meshes to right; bring it out 1 mesh directly to left.

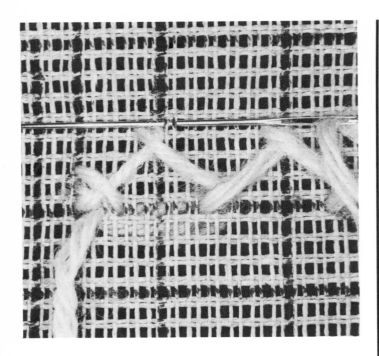

2—Insert needle 4 meshes above and 4 meshes to right (1 mesh to right of second stitch in Row 1); bring it out 1 mesh directly to left. Continue as in step *3* of Row 1.

2—Insert needle 4 meshes above and 4 meshes to right (1 mesh to right of second stitch in Row 2); bring it out 1 mesh directly to left. Continue as in step *3* of Row 1.

ROW 3, COLOR 2 (OR 3)
1—Bring needle through to front 1 mesh below top edge (1 mesh above first stitch in Row 2). Insert needle 3 meshes below and 3 meshes to right; bring it out 1 mesh directly to left.

ROW 4, COLOR 2 (OR 4)
1—Bring needle through to front through top mesh. Insert it 4 meshes below and 4 meshes to right; bring it out 1 mesh directly to left.

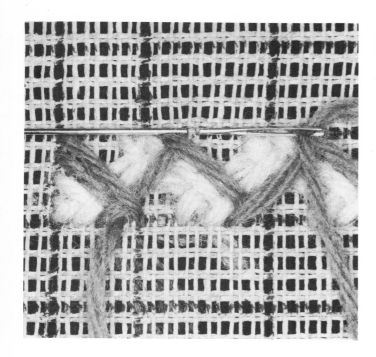

2—Insert needle 4 mashes above and 4 meshes to right (1 mesh to right of second stitch in Row 3), bring it out 1 mesh directly to left. Continue as in step *3* of Row 1.

2—Insert needle 4 meshes below and 4 meshes to right (1 mesh to right of second stitch in Row 4); bring it out 1 mesh directly to left. Continue as in step *2* of Row 1.

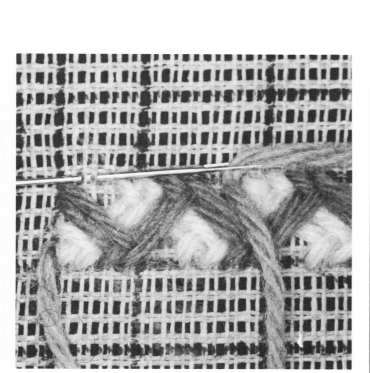

ROW 5, COLOR 3 (OR 5)

1—Go carefully here. Bring needle through to front 4 meshes below top edge. Insert it 4 meshes above and 2 meshes to right (2 meshes to right of first stitch in Row 4); bring it out 1 mesh directly to left.

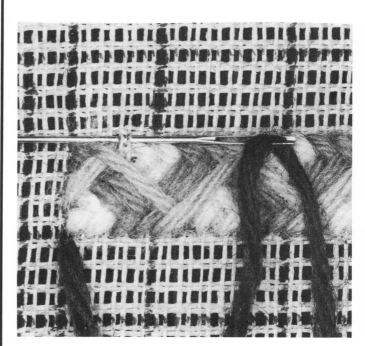

ROW 6, COLOR 4 (OR 6)

1—Bring needle through to front 5 meshes below top edge. Insert it 4 meshes above and 3 meshes to right (1 mesh to right of first stitch in Row 5); bring it out 1 mesh directly to left.

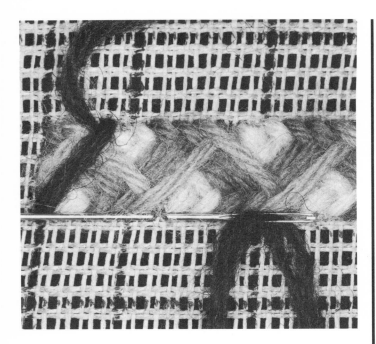

2—Insert needle 4 meshes below and 4 meshes to right (1 mesh to right of second stitch in Row 5—the only place you *can* put it!); bring it out 1 mesh directly to left. Continue as in step *2* of Row 1.

Herringbone #2

Herringbone #2 is worked exactly like Herringbone #1 for the first six rows. It is at the seventh row that the directions change.

ROWS 7-12
Repeat the first six rows.

ROW 7, COLOR 1
1—Starting at the left, bring needle through to front of canvas 3 meshes above bottom edge (1 mesh below completed band). Insert needle 1 mesh above and 1 mesh to right; bring it out 1 mesh directly to left.

2—Insert needle 4 meshes below and 4 meshes to right; bring it out 1 mesh directly to left.

ROW 8, COLOR 1 (OR 2)
1—Bring needle through to front 2 meshes above bottom edge (1 mesh below first stitch in Row 7). Insert needle 2 meshes above and 2 meshes to right; bring it out 1 mesh directly to left. Continue as in step 2 of Row 7.

3—Insert needle 4 meshes above and 4 meshes to right;. bring it out 1 mesh directly to left. To continue, repeat from step 2. To begin next row, proceed from step 3 as follows.

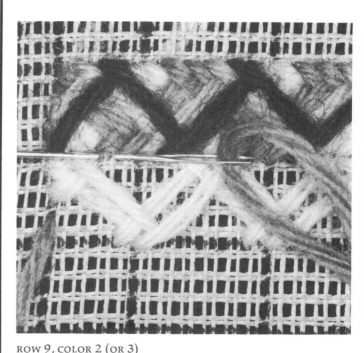

ROW 9, COLOR 2 (OR 3)
1—Bring needle through to front 1 mesh above bottom edge (1 mesh below first stitch in Row 8). Insert needle 3 meshes above and 3 meshes to right; bring it out 1 mesh directly to left. Continue as in step 2 of Row 7.

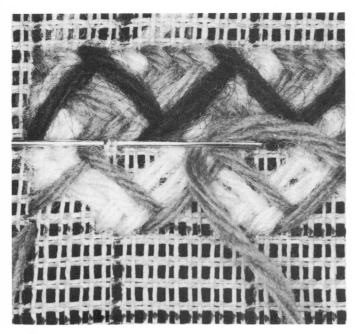

ROW 10, COLOR 2 (OR 4)

1—Bring needle through to front through bottom mesh. Insert it 4 meshes above and 4 meshes to right; bring it out 1 mesh directly to left. Continue as in step 2 of Row 7.

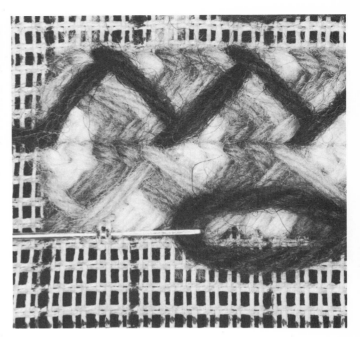

ROW 12, COLOR 4 (OR 6)

1—Bring needle through to front through 4 meshes above bottom edge (the same mesh as first stitch in Row 6). Insert needle 4 meshes below and 3 meshes to right; bring it out 1 mesh directly to left. Continue as in step *3* of Row 7.

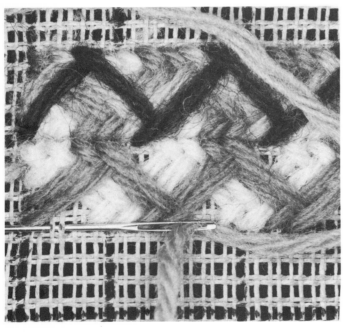

ROW 11, COLOR 3 (OR 5)

1—Bring needle through to front 3 meshes above bottom edge (1 mesh below first stitch in Row 7). Insert needle 3 meshes below and 2 meshes to right; bring it out 1 mesh directly to left. Continue as in step *3* of Row 7.

Fringe

There are a variety of ways to handle fringe, depending on the effect you want. Shown here is a fringe of silk and wool, with loops uncut; the following illustration shows a wool fringe with loops cut. The length of a fringe is a matter of choice. For an average-size pillow (about 12 by 14 inches), I like the loops at least an inch long.

The fringe given in the following pictures is very firm, and the knotting is not bulky. *You must work fringe from left to right.* It is easier to work from the bottom up; otherwise, the loops from the row above can get in your way. The number of rows and meshes between rows is a matter of choice: it depends on how full or scanty you want the fringe.

2—Holding the end of the yarn down with left thumb, insert needle 1 mesh above (the same mesh as first insertion); bring it out 1 mesh to left. Pull it firmly to secure the yarn.

1—Starting at the left, with needle and yarn in front of the canvas, insert needle and bring it out 1 mesh directly below.

3—Insert needle 1 mesh to right (again the same mesh as first insertion); bring it out 1 mesh below, leaving a loop of the desired length (I use my left thumb for measuring as I go along). Hold the loop in place with your thumb.

4—Insert needle 1 mesh to right; bring it out 1 mesh to left. Pull this top stitch firmly but not too tightly. (If you are working on mono-canvas, insert needle 2 meshes to right and bring it out 2 meshes to left.)

6—Row 2: again starting at the left, repeat from step *1*.

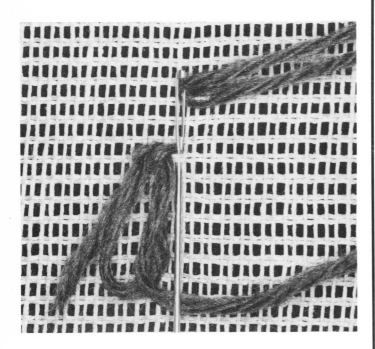

5—To continue, repeat from step *3*.

Bibliography

Dillmont, Therese de, *Encyclopedia of Needlework* (Editions Th. de Dillmont, no date)
Hanley, Hope, *Needlepoint* (Scribner, 1964)
Harbeson, Georgiana Brown, *American Needlework* (Bonanza, 1968)
Hughes, Therle, *English Domestic Needlework* (Macmillan, 1961)
McGown, Pearl K., *Color in Hooked Rugs* (McGown, 1954)
Williams, Elsa S., *Heritage Embroidery* (Reinhold, 1967)

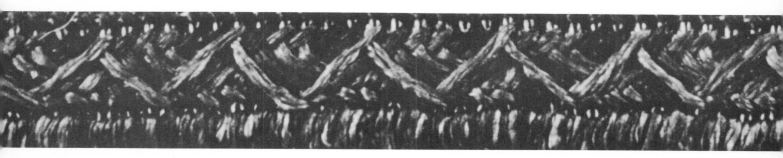

List of Suppliers

C. R. Meissner Co.
22 East 29th Street
New York, N.Y. 10016

Joan Toggitt Ltd.
1170 Broadway
New York, N.Y. 10001

Index of Stitches

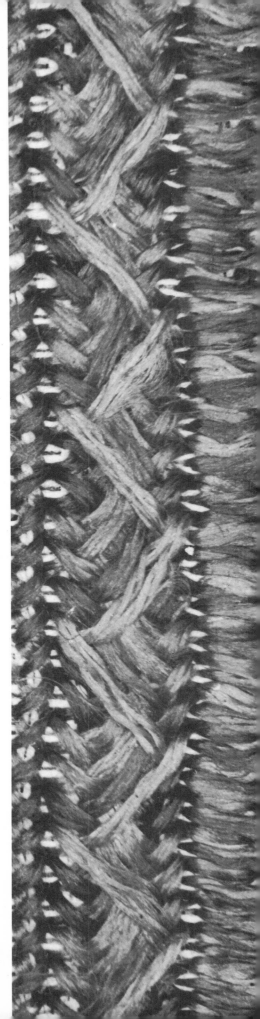